Fips, Bots, Doggeries, and More

To my favorite writer of book reviews — :)

Tracy Lawson

Fips, Bots, Doggeries, and More

Explorations of Henry Rogers' 1838 Journal of Travel from Southwestern Ohio to New York City

by

Tracy Lawson

The McDonald & Woodward Publishing Company
Granville, Ohio

The McDonald & Woodward Publishing Company
Granville, Ohio   www.mwpubco.com

Fips, Bots, Doggeries, and More: Explorations of Henry Rogers' 1838 Journal of Travel from Southwestern Ohio to New York City

Orignial text and selected figures © 2012 by Tracy Lawson

All rights reserved
Printed in the United States of America by McNaughton & Gunn, Inc., Saline, Michigan, on paper that meets the minimum requirements of permanence for printed library materials.

First Printing April 2012
10 9 8 7 6 5 4 3 2 1
20 19 18 17 16 15 14 13 12

Library of Congress Cataloging-in-Publication Data

Rogers, Henry, 1806-1896.
　Fips, bots, doggeries, and more : explorations of Henry Rogers' 1838 journal of travel from southwestern Ohio to New York City / Tracy Lawson.
　　　p. cm.
　Includes bibliographical references and index.
　ISBN 978-1-935778-19-6 (pbk. : alk. paper)
　1. Rogers, Henry, 1806-1896—Diaries. 2. Rogers, Henry, 1806-1896—Travel—Middle Atlantic States. 3. Rogers, Henry, 1806-1896—Travel—Ohio. 4. Travelers—Middle Atlantic States—Diaries. 5. Travelers—Ohio—Diaries. 6. Middle Atlantic States—Description and travel. 7. Ohio—Description and travel. 8. Lawson, Tracy, 1966—Travel—Middle Atlantic States. 9. Lawson, Tracy, 1966—Travel—Ohio. I. Lawson, Tracy, 1966- II. Title.
　F106.R75 2012
　917.71—dc23

2012011783

Reproduction or translation of any part of this work, except for short excerpts used in reviews, without the written permission of the copyright owner is unlawful. Requests for permission to reproduce parts of this work, or for additional information, should be addressed to the publisher.

Contents

Acknowledgments vii
Introduction 1
Prologue 7

Section I — 1838

Henry Rogers' Journal 13
   1. Starting Out 13
   2. Columbus 18
   3. Eastern Ohio 24
   4. Virginia and Western Pennsylvania 30
   5. Maryland 37
   6. Eastern Pennsylvania 44
   7. Trenton and Hunterdon County 48
   8. City Living 58
Expansions 69
Endnotes for Prologue and Section I 89

Section II — 2003–2009

Following in Henry's Footsteps 105
Epilogue 125
Appendixes 129
Bibliography 137
Index 145

Dedication

To Mom and Dad, who went the extra mile to get the copy of Henry's journal. Thanks for knowing just how much I would enjoy it.

To Bob, who said, "Of course you should."

And to Keri, who is the best daughter, sidekick, and research assistant I could ever want.
Thanks for coming along for the ride.

Acknowledgments

Marie Duquette was the first to say, "It's done — take it out of the oven already!" Thanks, Marie, for your unwavering support. May this be the first of many projects in our writing careers.

Kelly Thacher at Blue Door Editorial helped refine the final draft with sage advice and confidence-boosting enthusiasm. I dearly loved reconnecting with you, Kelly!

Chase Smith, himself a skillful and witty editor, assisted with the index and unsnarled 20 years' worth of bibliographical sources.

My great aunts, Winona Rogers Brigode and Florence Rogers Rieck, Henry Rogers' great-granddaughters, provided answers to my questions. I appreciate the time they spent with me and the joy with which they anticipated seeing a part of their family story in print.

Jerry McDonald and Trish Newcomb at McDonald & Woodward Publishing walked me through the editing and publication process for this, my first book. I appreciate their support and their wise suggestions, and for the way they treated me like family.

Additional help was provided by: Rose Brown, Librarian/Genealogist, Montgomery County Historical Society, Norristown, PA; Betty Burlingame, Rockn Bee

Farms, Torrington, WY; Robert E. Cluck, Adams County Historical Society, Gettysburg, PA; Joan Sellers Esterline, owner, Silver Fox Equestrian Center, Webberville, MI; Wayne Keefer, Hancock Historical Society and Museum, Hancock, MD; Becky Leamy, Librarian, Tri-County Heritage Society, Morgantown, PA; Judith Lowther, owner, Historic Smith House Antiques and Collectibles, Mount Sterling, OH; Carl McIlroy, East Vincent Township Historical Commission, Chester County, PA; Kelly McEntee, Inkeeper, Fairfield Inn, Fairfield, PA; Catherine Medich, archivist, New Jersey State Archives, Trenton, NJ; James Neville, Executive Director, Washington County Historical Society, Hancock, MD; Cassandra Pritts, Allegany County Historical Society, Cumberland, MD; Barbara Raid, Historic York, York, PA; Robin Schuricht, Ohio Historical Society, Columbus, OH; Kristen Stauffer, Lancaster York Heritage Region, Wrightsville, PA; Martha Tykodi, West Licking Historical Society, Licking County, OH; Charles R. Virts, Curator, Champaign Historical Museum, Urbana, OH; David Wiles, Clear Spring Historical Association, Clear Spring, MD; and Brenda Wolfe, Muskingum County Genealogical Society, Zanesville, OH, all of whom I thank.

Introduction

Henry Rogers, a miller and my great-great-great-grandfather, along with his wife and her parents, took a wagon trip from Mount Pleasant, Ohio, to New York City and then back to Ohio in the summer and fall of 1838. This was a working vacation on which the party visited family, did some sightseeing, toured numerous mills to observe ways to improve their own milling business, and witnessed numerous ways in which the world they knew in southwestern Ohio was changing. Henry, who was 32 years old at the time, is believed to have kept a daily journal of the entire trip, but only the portion of the journal covering the journey from Mount Pleasant to the arrival in New York City is known to have survived.

Early in his journal, Henry states that his intention "is . . . to mention all interesting subjects and things that come under my observation," and, true to this statement, his record of the journey contains a rich diversity of observations of and thoughts about the natural and cultural landscapes through which he and his party passed. The long list of things that attracted his interest included landforms, waterways, and natural vegetation; soils, crops, livestock, barns, and other elements of the agricultural landscape; transportation facilities such as roads, canals, bridges, and railroads; inns, hotels, and other travelers' services; growing towns and their evolving businesses and institutions; and the social, political, economic, and religious environment which made up large parts of Henry's world. Expenses, illnesses of both the people and one of their horses, and visits with the many friends and family were also recorded.

In summary, Henry's travelogue is a firsthand account of a literate businessman who travelled from the youthful Midwest frontier to the maturing heartland of the United States at a time that the innovations of the Agricultural and Industrial revolutions were bringing about rapid change in America.

The Journal and Me

In 1990, when I was researching my family's history, my parents thought I'd enjoy reading Henry's journal. They contacted my father's Aunt Nonie and asked to borrow her typewritten transcript of the original document. She refused to lend it, fearing it would be lost if she put it in the mail. Undeterred, my parents loaded a photocopier in their car and drove from their home in Cincinnati to Elida, Ohio, to copy the journal at Aunt Nonie's dining-room table. They surprised me with the copy of the journal that Christmas. It was a wonderful gift. Reading it then, and many times since, has inspired me to make my own journeys — of different sorts and at different times — following the same route taken by Henry and his family.

Traveling by horse and wagon, Henry's party interacted with many people along the way. They asked questions about local commerce, crops, railroads, and mechanical innovations. Henry kept careful notes about everything he observed and learned. He also recorded the cost of meals, lodging, and other expenses, and even ruefully reported his tendency to fall asleep in church.

I had always planned to write a book, and after I read Henry's journal a few times, I started thinking about ways to use his story in my own writing endeavors. I considered selecting details from the journal to use in a fiction piece, but I didn't know enough about his world or his times to write about them accurately, so I started researching those places, events, and circumstances. Soon, this research became my focus. I was driven to learn about everything Henry described in his journal, partly because he was my ancestor, and partly because the information in the journal was so diverse, yet interrelated. I came to realize that his journal might be of value and interest to others, especially if it were published in its entirety. I decided to do just that and write a book focused on Henry's journal, but I wanted to supplement that focus with some of the additional information I had collected in order to provide the reader with a greater understanding of what it might have been like to have lived and traveled in America in 1838.

I started my research using state archives, public libraries, and the primitive early Internet to explore broad topics related to the journal. I studied how water-powered mills work and toured several 19th-Century mills in Ohio, and in doing so gained great respect for my ancestor's mechanical and carpentry skills. Dress, travel, and medicine of the period were other subjects that aroused my interest. Because improving the country's infrastructure was a matter of great public concern at the time, I acquainted myself with the need for, the importance of, and the politics behind the development of Ohio's canal system and the National Road.

I consulted with the caretaker of a cemetery in rural eastern Pennsylvania because Henry seemed particularly moved by the plight of the Revolutionary soldiers buried there. I discussed milling terminology with a millwright in Garrettsville, Ohio. I dispatched my sister, who was studying at the University of Pennsylvania, to discover the name and service record of a ship that was under construction in the Philadelphia Navy Yard at the time of Henry's visit, and which Henry had described in great detail. These discoveries and others made

Introduction

Henry's journal, and his world, so real to me. To be sure, things had changed since 1838, but, as I came to realize, much of Henry's world still existed in mine. Did he ever dream his writings would be read, examined, and studied with such pleasure and excitement more than 150 years after he created them?

A Plan Emerges

As I continued to delve into Henry's journal and world, I increasingly wanted to tell his story — but I wasn't sure how to do it. My study of the journal took a back seat for several years while I started a small business, and then had a child. But when we moved to Columbus, Ohio, in 1996, our home was three blocks south of the National Road, and that proximity to a road Henry had actually traveled on renewed my interest in the project. I worked on it when I could, but still I searched for a definitive way to tell the story. Several more years slipped by.

When I took Henry's journal to the National Road Festival in Addison, Pennsylvania, in May, 2003, I had planned to make some notes about the area while my husband's base ball team, the Ohio Village Muffins, played in a vintage base ball tournament — base ball was spelled as two words in the 19th Century. The weather was extremely cold and drizzly, so I spent a good portion of the weekend keeping warm in the village shops. I also toured the toll house on the old section of the National Road — and did so thoughtfully, knowing it was a tangible link to Henry and his story. In part because of this visit, I came to realize I that needed to see and explore the land that Henry traversed in a way that would allow me to parallel Henry's experience.

On the way home, I said to my husband, "I need to drive the entire distance, like Henry did." To his credit, he immediately said, "Of course you do." I would travel with Keri, our eight-year-old daughter. Henry's story could be *our* story! I had new resolve, new direction; I began planning our trip.

To prepare for my and Keri's journey, I re-read Henry's journal and made lists of every place he mentioned in the first half of the journal, wondering if — perhaps even hoping that — I would find some of them unchanged. I packed reproductions of maps from the 1830s and 40s as well as a current road atlas so I could make comparisons among them and choose the routes that seemed to best follow Henry's path. I planned to stop at county courthouses, cemeteries, and historical societies to undertake even more field research. I hoped most of all to find personal details about the people mentioned in Henry's journal.

Even though I was determined to maximize my efficiency, I left one detail unplanned: I did not book any hotels in advance. I wanted us to be free to travel with flexibility.

Later that summer of 2003, Keri and I traveled from Mount Healthy, formerly Henry's Mount Pleasant, Ohio, to Leitersburg, Maryland, in air-conditioned comfort, armed with maps, notebooks, and camera. In August, 2004, we picked up where we had left off in Leitersburg and drove the rest of the way to Philadelphia, Pennsylvania. In May, 2009, I flew to Philadelphia and spent additional time there and across the Delaware River in the family's hometown of Trenton, New Jersey.

A Note on the Authenticity of the Journal

Henry's original, handwritten journal is lost to the ages. I tried to track it down, but to no avail, and I shudder to think that someone in the family who didn't realize its value discarded it. Without the original document being available, the typewritten copy of Henry's journal was, to some degree, suspect. At best, I realized it might contain transcription errors or omissions, and at worst, it could be a complete fabrication.

As I studied and researched the people and places Henry mentioned in the journal, however, almost all the details clearly fit together with the geographical and historical record of the time and place covered by the document. I quickly became convinced that the journal really was a product of the journey it described. I noted some misspellings, but it was unclear whether the misspellings were Henry's, or if the typist had misread his handwriting. The less-obvious misspellings complicated my fact checking. For example, one of Henry's journal entries had been transcribed to read:

From hence to Norristown and thence to the Sign of the Broadacre Tavern 6 miles from Norristown kept by Mrs. Cuff.

There we put up for the night.

Unable to confirm the existence of a tavern by that name, I sought help from Rose Brown of the Historical Society of Montgomery County, Pennsylvania, who responded to my query:

Dear Mrs. Lawson:

I believe that the BROADACRE refers to the Broad Axe Tavern and it is still located at Skippack & Butler Pikes, in Whitpain Township outside Norristown. I have been searching for Mrs. Cuff of 1838, without results. There are no Cuffs listed in the 1840 Census for PA.

Then, ten days later, Rose emailed again:

I finally had a breakthrough. After Cuff's did not show up in the 1840 Census, I checked Cuffs through the deeds without luck. I read all I could find about the Broad Axe Tavern trying to trace the deeds through that information without luck. Then I looked at Whitpain Township tax records for 1838, and while reading every name I found Ann ACUFF, Innkeeper, with the caption under her name "& John Rex, est."Ann is listed in the spring and fall of 1838 and also in 1839.

Rose's research, which confirmed that Ann Acuff was an innkeeper in Whitpain Township in 1838 and 1839, was sufficient to validate and correct Henry's journal entry.

As I continued to research and resolve similar questions, I became confident that the information in the journal was accurate, except for occasional spelling errors. The text of the journal printed herein retains the spelling that appears in the typed copy with which I worked, except when proper names or names of places were misspelled. When I tried but could not substantiate a detail in the journal, I have provided an endnote indicating that no corroborating information was found.

Roadmap for the Reader

When I was done retracing Henry's journey, it was time to weave our stories together. Henry's journal is presented in its known entirety in Section I of this book. The first mentions of people, towns, and significant sites along the journey appear in boldface type. On a few occasions, I have inserted supplemental information in brackets to clarify the meaning of a word or words in the journal or other documents that might be unclear. Sidebars to the journal elaborate on unfamiliar terms and create a deeper awareness of what it was like to live in America early in the Victorian era. Vintage postcards and photographs help set the scene, even though they are all from a later period, and therefore cannot fully and accurately depict what Henry saw on his trip. That said, the landforms and waterways across which Henry journeyed are still where they were in 1838. And, some of the same structures remain that Henry visited, while others have been replaced by more modern structures that fulfill the same purpose their predecessors did in Henry's day.

In the Expansions part of Section I, I present a more in-depth look at topics related to Henry's time and experiences, including flour mills, politics, fashion, and folk medicine. Section II contains recollections of, and reflections upon, my three trips. Appendix I is a record of Henry's reported expenses, and Appendix II lists all family members mentioned in Henry's journal, their relationship to him, and their birth, death, and marriage data when available.

Prologue

Family, Home, and Business

In 1806, Henry Rogers, Sr., and his wife, Phoebe Burnett Rogers, moved their family, including their infant son, Henry, Jr., from Fayette County in western Pennsylvania to Hamilton County in southwestern Ohio. Henry, Sr., was a Revolutionary War veteran and a weaver by trade.

Young Henry grew up in Hamilton County, where he received an education typical for a frontier boy.[1] At age 17, Henry apprenticed to a cabinetmaker but decided the trade was not to his liking, and by 1828 he was working for Jediah Hill on his farm and in his sawmill.

Jediah Hill was born in 1793 in New Jersey, and had migrated to Hamilton County, Ohio, in 1819, with his wife Eliza Hendrickson Hill and their three-year-old daughter, Rachel Maria. The Hills settled in Mount Pleasant, on the west fork of Mill Creek. (The village was renamed Mount Healthy after it was spared the devastation of a cholera epidemic in 1850.) Jediah built shelter for his young family by cutting down a large tree and constructing a cabin around the remaining stump — which the family used as a table. Jediah built a sawmill in 1820 and sold lumber to settlers in the surrounding area.

Jediah prospered. He built a farmhouse on the hill above the mill with a well in the basement and closets in the upstairs bedrooms. Rachel Maria Hill and Henry Rogers, Jr., married in 1832. Some six years later, the two — along with Rachel's mother and father — made the journey to New York City and

Figure 1. The Hill-Rogers homestead, built around 1840, as it appeared in the 1990s.

Figure 2. Mount Healthy Mill and the Hill-Rogers homestead alongside Mill Creek in Mount Healthy, Ohio.

back, the first part of which is detailed in that portion of Henry's journal that follows.

Jediah and Henry built a covered bridge over Mill Creek in 1850, at which time Henry and Rachel's seven-year-old son, Wilson, made the ceremonial first crossing of the bridge in his dog cart. Over the years, the family continued to build up the farm and the milling business.

In 1887, when he was 81 years old, Henry and his son Wilson sold the mill to Charles Hartman, Sr. The Rogers family kept the farm, and Wilson also worked at the post office. Hartman converted the mill for exclusive use as a gristmill, chose the name "Pride of the Valley" for his flour, and built a new house near the mill.

Charles Hartman sold the mill to C. C. Groff in 1911. During Mr. Groff's ownership, he converted the mill to steam power, and later to diesel. At the peak of its production, the mill could produce 150 hundred-pound sacks of cake flour a day and served more than 300 bakers, restaurants, hotels, and

Prologue

Figure 3. Mount Healthy Mill after it ceased operations.

Figure 4. The last photo of the mill was taken in October, 1981, just days before the structure was destroyed by fire.

other customers in the Cincinnati area. The product was known as "El-Mi-Jo" Flour, named for Groff's daughters Elaine, Miriam, and Joan.

The Army Corps of Engineers bought the mill in 1952 as part of the Mill Creek Flood Control project. The mill stood empty for nearly three decades, stripped of its equipment, deteriorating, and subject to vandalism. Hamilton County Parks initiated plans to restore the mill, but in October, 1981, an arsonist set fire to the 161-year-old structure, and it burned to the ground in less than an hour. Kevin Hardwick, a fire fighter on the scene in 1981 and the owner of the Hill/Rogers homestead, said that light from the flames could be seen in downtown Cincinnati, twelve miles away.

Members of the Rogers family occupied the homestead until 1970. The house is now privately owned and lovingly cared for by Kevin and Cindy Hardwick who refer to it as their "money pit." If you look carefully in the woods near the creek, some foundation stones from the mill are still there, hidden in the underbrush.

Section I

1838

Henry Rogers' Journal

1

Starting Out

Started from home on the 18th of August, went through **Springdale**, **Chester** and **Union Village** to **William Anderson's**.[2]

Sunday 19th, stayed at Anderson's.

Monday, 20th, left for **Dayton** a quarter past 6, passed through **Centreville** at 7, arrived in Dayton a quarter before 9. Left at half past 9. Arrived at **J. Duer's**[3] at 12 o clock. Left J. Duer's at 3 and arrived at **William Hart's**[4] at half past 5.

Tuesday morning, 21st, after making some observations about William Hart's farm, came to where there was a mill dam made of nigger heads, went back to the house, loaded up and put out at 10 o'clock.

Arrived at **Fletcher** at 12. Put up at **Wharton's**.[5] Saw **Aunt Charlotte Duer**.[6] Her health is quite impaired. The rest of our friends were all well in this place. This day's travel was through a very fertile country, abounding in springs of running water. The prospect of corn is tolerably good. The country is new yet, there is also a variety of timber, such as beech, ash, poplar, oak, butternut, walnut, hickory and diverse others. The country is tolerably level, rather inclining in some places to lie marshy. The soil is of a chocolate color and very rich. There seems to

> John Eagley, historian at Hopkins Old Water Mill in Garrettsville, Ohio, explained to the author in 1991 that "nigger heads" is a vernacular term for round granite stones, 10–24 inches in diameter, and ranging in color from red to gray to blue. These stones make good foundations for smaller buildings, are extremely hard, and are suitable for making millstones.

Fred Archer, in *The Countryman Cottage Life Book*, writes:

"[We determined] the size of an iron tyre by 'running the wheel' with an iron disc and counting the revolutions as the disc ran round the wheel. This looked simple but was highly skilled; you could wobble the disc and get quite the wrong measurement. We got down strips of iron and cut off the right lengths, allowing for the weld. We warmed each strip in the fire and hammered it into a circle, first cutting and tapering forks in the ends of the weld. While he put the finishing touches to the tyre, I rolled the wheel to the wheel-pit, where I laid it down, the huge hub resting in a central depression and the rim on the brick circle.

"The smith shifted the tyre round in the fire until the iron was red hot. Then seizing the glowing circle with tongs, we lowered it into position round the wheel, helping it down with one or two blows from a sledge. Clouds of steam rose as we shrank and hardened the tyre with bucket of water. Lastly nails were driven through holes into the felloes [wooden rim sections], and the job was done."

be generally some of the best livers through these parts. Good houses and barns seem to be reared on the farms generally. We left Fletcher at half past 5 and arrived at **Enoch Drake's**[7] about sunset. He lives about three miles east and one north of Fletcher. The road from Fletcher to Drake's is considerably rail-roady and very rough. Here we got some bewildered and Mother Hill and myself went until within sight of the house and then I went back to pilot the wagon in. All landed safe. Found **Aunt Rachel** with a very sick headache, the rest of the family were all well.

Wednesday morning, 22nd, fine clear and pleasant morning. All well this morning. I started to **George Suber's**[8] on foot while Aunt Rachel, Maria and Father and Mother Hill came in the wagon. Found **Uncle James Anderson**[9] here. Went all together to Uncle **David Anderson's**,[10] here we saw **Peter, Joseph, David and Daniel Anderson**[11] with **George Worthington**[12] and his **wife**. George made and set a shoe on Charley [one of the horses] and him and Daniel cut and set the tyres[13] on the hind wheels of the wagon. At evening, all started together for Suber's. Here we left Uncle James, **Aunt Deborah**,[14] and **Ephriam Anderson**[15] and his wife. They went on down the country and we to Enoch Drake's. This part of the country is remarkably well timbered. I went this day to a White Oak tree that measured 21 ft. round, 4 ft. from the ground and carried it's thickness to the height of probably 80 ft. Poplar timber is generally the handsomest I have seen. The corn in this part of the country is very good. Fruit scarce, potatoes are not very prosperous.

Thursday morning 23rd. Clear and pleasant and all well. We went out this morning with Mr. Drake to look over his farm, which is first rate stock, water is not so plenty on this nor any of the adjoining farms as there is down south. We rambled more til noon and then we all went to see a **Mr. Asa Scott**,[16] where we were most agreeably entertained and feasted on melons. Looked around over Mr.

Henry's Journal — Starting Out

Scott's corn and other things and found that he had a very flattering prospect of reaping the fruits of his labor. After we had participated in drinking tea, we returned to Mr. Drake's in the evening. Some signs of rain, but seems to be passing away.

Friday 24th, pleasant. All well except Mother Hill complains of the headache. Preparing now to start our journey after breakfast. We took leave of all the family and started about 7 o'clock. Steering our course for Columbus, passing through **Elizabeth town, Paris, Westville** and **Urbana** by 12 o'clock. The forenoon has been tolerably warm and dusty. We passed by a mill[17] on a stream which we took to be a branch of the Mad River between Westville and Paris and then another saw and grinding establishment[18] on the main stream. Then a beautiful piece of prairie just before we got into Urbana, stretching north and south of the road to a considerable extent, then we came in sight of Urbana. Here we halted a few minutes, watered our horses and in the meantime I went into the bank of Urbana and presented a few shin plasters[19] to have exchanged, which they done with good grace. I must have remarked that if I had not saw the small sign on the door "bank open" I should have thought I was going into a dogery.[20]

Evening, Maria and Mother both have sick headache, very bad. There is some prospects of a shower this evening. This day's travel has been through a great deal of prairie land,[21] so flat and low that it cannot be cultivated and what little timber there has been is principally burr oak and scrubby at that, with hazel bushes as thick as they can stand almost all over the ground. In the fore part of the day we had lots of railroad[22] to travel over—which is not very easy neither for the wagon, man or horse.

Between **Mechanicsburg** and **Jefferson** there is not in the distance of 18 miles, one public house where there is any chance of entertainment. A[t] about dusk we arrived in the town of Jefferson and put up at A. Winchester's hotel[23]

Shinplasters were paper money of low denomination which circulated in the frontier economies from 1837–1863. Shinplasters issued by banks, merchants, wealthy individuals, and associations as IOUs were intended to alleviate the shortage of small change in growing frontier regions caused by the Specie Circular Act of 1836. Henry must have been pleasantly surprised to find the Bank of Urbana willing to exchange its shinplasters for coin!

By railroad, Henry means a corduroy road, which consisted of split logs laid in the roadbed perpendicular to the long axis, or direction, of the road.

Figure 5. The "tyres" on wagon wheels had to be replaced by a blacksmith several times during a journey like Henry's.

Figure 6. The tail race from Hunter's Mill, Urbana, Ohio.

Figure 7. Construction of the National Road through Jefferson, Ohio, began in 1830 and was completed in 1834.

where we were hospitably received and everything done to make us comfortable. 8 o'clock, and suppertime. The women are much better, so that they drank a little tea and eat some.

    To conclude the remarks of this days travel, I would say that we have come through a very poor part of the country. The soil is generally thin with a gravelly bottom. In some of the prairie there seems to be an abundance of hay put up and considerable number of cattle ranging the forests. Corn on average is very light, and here is but a very small portion of the land cultivated from Mechanicsburg to Jefferson. I have noticed but very little wheat and that appears to be quite light.

Henry Rogers' Journal

2

Columbus

Saturday morning 25th, clear and pleasant. We all appear to be considerably better. We have put on our blacked boots this morning and called for our breakfast and are at this time looking over some Whig papers. I believe our host is a Whig from the quantity of Whig Papers he has about his house. After breakfast we settled up our bill, which was $2.50 and left Jefferson at 7. Passed through **Alton** and **Frankfort** [sic: Franklinton] to **Columbus**.

We got into Columbus at 10 o'clock am and soon found **Mr. Levi B. Pinney's**[24] residence where we stopped for the day. This day's travel has been on the National Road,[25] which runs about an east course. We crossed first a stream called the Little Darby and then Big Darby. The bridges over these two streams are of the most elegant structure. The stone masonry is out of lime-stone of the best sort and averages from 8 to 18 inches thick. The one across the Scioto is different in structure from the other two, it being made in two reaches, a splendid stone pier in the center. There are besides the wagon tracks a walk on each side of the bridge for foot people. As it is my intention to mention all interesting subjects and things that come under my observation, I will endeavor to describe our course while in this place.

Figure 8. High Street, Columbus, Ohio, from a postcard dated 1904. Columbus' service-oriented economy is an outgrowth of the city's early role as a transportation hub, which encouraged wholesale trade rather than industry.

Henry's Journal — Columbus

Here I will remark that about 3 o'clock there was a most horrid uproar broke out in a grocery (or rather a dogery, for it seemed to be a resort for scoundrels and topers[26]) a man, or a brute in the shape of a man, got quite addled in his upper story and wanted to fight some one or other of the company, the landlord all the while trying to pacify him, but all to no purpose. He at length, like a smothered fire, lighted up in a most awful blaze, burst out in a most frightful manner—and he cleared the house instantly of all that was in, both furniture of the house, such as chairs, barrels, pitchers and tumblers, staving everything to atoms that he got into his hands and it seemed as if the infernal regions was opened and some of the inmates let loose. The fiendish yells that proceeded from the house was terrible for the space of 15 or 20 minutes.

When he emerged from the house with his pack on his back, thinking to make his escape from justice, the crowd was too much exasperated to let the villain go. One more daring than the rest stepped up and gave him a severe blow on the head, and brought him to a settlement. In the meantime the landlord had gone and got the marshal of the city and had him arrested. Just about the time that the fellow knocked him down he was taken before the mayor and fined $5.00 and sentenced to six days imprisonment. We had about this time a most delightful shower of rain which cooled the air and laid the dust and rendered it far more agreeable and pleasant.

At about 4 o'clock, Father and Mother Hill, Maria and myself and **Miss Hannah Burge**[27] started to visit the state prison[28] and got caught in a shower of rain just as we got to the prison walls. We passed through the large iron gate and there we received 5 blank tickets. We were then told to go to the office where we paid 25 cents a piece for the men and 12½ cents a piece for the women. There we received 5 more tickets with the word admit on it. We then proceeded to the keeper of the iron door which is right in the center of the prison, between the east

My husband's favorite passage in Henry's journal is the description of the drunken man in the Columbus saloon; Bob likes how the man was apprehended with a stunning blow, immediately taken before the mayor, fined and imprisoned, just like that. Swift and efficient justice on a Saturday afternoon. I wonder if Henry was intrigued or appalled by the drunken man's tirade, and how it colored his opinion of Columbus! Henry doesn't appear to have been a drinker himself, and he comments a couple times on the "scoundrels and topers" he encountered at different taverns. I loved the way Henry ended the story metaphorically, by commenting on the "shower of rain that cooled the air and rendered it far more agreeable and pleasant".

The Ohio Penitentiary, located at the corner of Spring Street and Neil Avenue, was constructed between 1832 and 1834, with additions in 1835 and 1837, all built with convict labor.

Local companies hired prisoners to perform skilled labor, and the prisoners' manufactured items were sold or exchanged for provisions or raw materials. Major reforms in the prison system in the 1830s sought to reward good behavior and let "kindness and humane treatment" substitute for some of the more rigid rules.

Under these reforms, prisoners were paid for their labors, and many returned to society with money enough to establish themselves in the field of their choosing. Illiterate prisoners were required to attend night classes and all prisoners took part in religious services each Sunday.

This first attempt at convict rehabilitation, combined with humane treatment, was considered successful, measured by the cooperation and morale of the prisoners.

---

and west wings, with two other doors of the same as that of the first. The keeper opened the first door and waited until we had gotten through, then we were let through the other door into the west wing, which is four stories high, with cells not more than 4 or 5 feet apart and a strong iron grate for every cell, through which light is communicated and no other.

After passing through the hall the next place was a room in which lace girting[29] and everything belonging to coaches, carriages, etc. was manufactured, together with stirrups, bridle bits and plated iron of every description, and that too of the neatest kind. This department is conducted by Hayden & Co., who pays the state for the use of the prisoners. The next place we visited was their dining room. This place is so arranged that none of the prisoners sit facing each other. There are 12 companies of prisoners and one guard for each company. When dinner is ready, the bell rings and they all come in without any ceremony and take their seats. When the bell rings (so we were informed for we did not see) they all at the same time pull off their hats, then another toll of the bell and they all fall to eating and then are dismissed the same way.

The next was the saddle making which is carried on very extensively. The next was the blacksmiths who were very diligently at work. The next was the coopers.[30] This department is carried on by a man by the name of Piney, and he also hires the prisoners from the state. The establishment is very profitable. The next was the stone cutters who was employed in cutting stone for a new court house and Hall. The next was the shoemakers and tailors. The tailors are also hired from the state by Hurdell & Co. Merchant Tailors. I have missed one or two departments which was next to the lace department. That was the washing and cooking and baking rooms, all of which is kept in the best kind of order and very clean.

The prisoners are called out by companies according to their number, and they form in single file, the tallest men in front as close as they can stand. At the word, they all step off together—this is the manner in which they go to dinner, from dinner to their cells, or from them. The discipline of the prisoners is such that not one of them are allowed to speak or look at one another. If they do break over the rules of the prison they are sure to be caught, for there is a guard or two placed in every department of the prison. They are informed on, are brought up and thrashed according to the crime without ever making any question, and then sent back to work.

After visiting the prison, I saw two fire, or water, engines, testing their strength in throwing water. They were about equal in power. They threw water over the steeple of the State House. Father Hill and I went down the river to the dam that feeds the canal. Our horses we put up at **Cadwallader's Hotel**.[31]

Sunday morning, 26th, is very clear, cool and pleasant. Got our horses and carriage and Father and Mother Hill, with Maria and **Mrs. Pinney**, took a ride, then after they got back and our horses put up again, we went to the **Baptist Church** and heard a sermon by a **Mr. Cressey**,[32] and again in the afternoon to the **Presbyterian** house[33] and a **Mr. Hoge** addressed the audience. The balance of the day was put in by walking out through the town and sitting about the house in friendly intercourse.

The town of Columbus is beautifully situated on an elevated piece of ground near the center of Franklin County, Ohio on the Scioto River. The town is not very compact, but very much detached, spreading over a large portion of the country and appears to be doing a considerable deal of improvement besides numerous dwellings and warehouses. There are three asylums,[34] one of which is finished for the deaf and dumb. The other two are not finished. The one for the lunatics is a most splendid building situated on the north east part of the town, as near as I was

Figure 9. Old First Presbyterian Church, located on Bryden Road in Columbus, Ohio.

Reverend Mr. Cressey came from the east as a missionary around 1834 and was soon the regular pastor at the Baptist Church in Columbus. He also served as a school examiner from 1838–1845.

The First Presbyterian Church of Columbus was founded in 1806. Reverend James Hoge, a missionary, formed the original church and remained its pastor until 1857.

Figure 10. Ohio Penitentiary, located at the corner of Spring Street and Neil Avenue, was constructed between 1832 and 1834, with additions in 1835 and 1837, all built with convict labor.

ASYLUM FOR THE DEAF AND DUMB, 1846.

ASYLUM FOR THE INSANE, 1846.

ASYLUM FOR THE BLIND, 1846.

Figure 11. Scene of inmates walking in lockstep at the Ohio Penitentiary.

Figure 12. Asylums in Columbus, Ohio.

capable of judging. It is about 350 ft. in length and four stories high. There are two rows of rooms in each wing, there being an east and a west wing. These rooms are about 10 ft. square, making about 80 rooms in each wing. Then there is a large hall through each wing, running the whole length of the building. Then there is another calculated for the blind, situated about an east course from the town. This is not as large as the lunatic asylum. I had not an opportunity of making any close discovery or examination. The lunatic asylum is built almost entirely by the prisoners. They have burned the brick, cut the stone and laid up the building, and do a considerable portion of the carpenter work. There is a large picket fence running around the building and about 5 guards stationed to keep order.

The Ohio Deaf and Dumb Asylum was erected in 1833–1834, a half mile east of the Statehouse. The pupils remained at the school for four to nine years, and were taught the manual alphabet along with academic subjects. The Asylum was the first of its kind in the Northwest Territory.

The Ohio Lunatic Asylum was finished in 1838, and built entirely at the expense of the state, and with convict labor, at a cost of $80,000. The Asylum could accommodate 145 patients and the attendants necessary to care for them.

The Ohio Institution for the Education of the Blind, after occupying temporary quarters on Town Street, moved to its five-story brick structure on the National Road in October 1839. The Institution offered a five year course of study in academics, and also various trades and occupations. Rev. Dr. James Hoge, N. D. Swayne, Esq., And Dr. William M. Awl were the first trustees charged with organizing the school.

Henry Rogers' Journal

Eastern Ohio

Monday morning 27th, clear and cool and pleasant and all well. We prepared for a start. The bill for keeping the horses during our stay in Columbus was $2.25. We came on the National Road 1 mile west of Jefferson, and after going one mile east came upon a toll gate where we paid 31½ cents and so on every 10 miles a gate where the same amount was charged. Our travels this day was through different qualities of soil.[35] The fore part of the day was through quite level country, with very little improvements of any description. We have passed this forenoon through the towns of **Hibernia**, situated on Big Walnut Creek, **Reynoldsburg**, **Havana**, **Etna** and **Kirkersville**, situated on the west side of the south branch of Licking River in Licking County. There is a grist mill and saw mill on the east side of the stream.[36] The mills are both drove with action and reaction percushion wheels.[37] They are of cast iron exclusively and are calculated to run under water when it backed up to a considerable height. At about 12, we stopped and fed and rested a while and then pursued our journey. The water in this part of the country is very sulphery, so that we cannot drink it. In the afternoon we came through towns of **Luray**, **Hebron**, **Jacksontown**, **Linville**, **Gratiot**, **Hopewell** and

Figure 13. All National Road markers, such as this one in eastern Ohio, showed the distance the marker was west of Cumberland, Maryland, and the distances to selected towns to the east and to the west of the marker.

Mt. Sterling,[38] where we put up. The town of Hebron is situated on the Ohio canal and appears to be doing some business.

The first gate we passed on the National Road,[39] there was an elderly lady came out and received the toll. The next was a man that had lost his nose, the next was a man with a wooden leg, the next was a man that had one hand off at the wrist and the other had the thumb turned back. The next was an old Jacksonian[40] and the next was a woman. These include all from Saturday to Monday evening.

We have come this afternoon to the hills east of the Licking summit. Here the National Road winds in various directions to get up and down these terrific hills and is from 2 to 3 degrees and through some very deep cuts, some as much as 20 or 25 ft. and that through a kind of freestone. These hills are very long. We have come to where there appears to be a considerable quantity of chestnut timber. The large trees are full of burrs. The corn in this days' travel is light. There appears to be a very large amount of small grain raised. After we came into the hilly country the land appears to be quite thin. About half of this day has been very dusty. About 4 miles from where we put up there was a shower of rain overtook us and laid the dust. We got to Mt. Sterling about sunset and put up at **Mr. Smith's** exchange, where we were tolerably entertained. It rained a little through the night. Bill $2.

Tuesday morning 28th. We are all well this morning except myself. I have a little boil on my arm. It looks cloudy and begins to rain. We started this morning for **Zanesville** for breakfast and it rained most of the way. We stopped at **C & T Rogers Hotel**[41] and stage office. Zanesville is in Muskingum County. We got our breakfast and then stepped out to look around. Made some discoveries.

The town of **Putnam** is on the west side and below the forks of the river. The bridge across the river is below the forks and is forked.[42] In the center of the bridge there are two gates. One goes to Zanesville and the other across what is

The groundbreaking for Ohio's segment of the National Road took place on July 4, 1825, in Saint Clairsville, Ohio. Coincidentally, the groundbreaking for the Ohio and Erie Canal was on the same day, four miles north of Hebron, Ohio. As a result, Hebron was located at an important transportation and commercial crossroads.

Figure 14. Mr. Edward Smith's tavern is located just west of Zanesville on US Route 40. The large, cut stone building is currently an antique store. The original portion of the tavern was built in 1830.

Figure 15. Y Bridge and Cassel Mill, Zanesville, Ohio.

Figure 16. Beaumont Mill, Zanesville, Ohio, 1875.

Figure 17. Hook Brothers & Aston Mill at Licking River Dam, Zanesville, Ohio.

Figure 18. Muskingum River Dam, Zanesville, Ohio.

called the little Licking Creek. This is a toll bridge. Our toll was 31½ cents. This is the greatest town for business I have passed through since I left home. There is three flour mills, two of which we were in. They have 6 pairs of stones each. There is also a very extensive manufactory of some sort or other on the Putnam side that is taken out of the Little Muskingum.

There are dams across the Big Muskingum, one of which is not finished. This one is a great display of architecture and is now in successful operation. The object of the second dam is first, because the old one is getting weak and second, to make slack water navigation up the river to Dresden where the [Ohio] canal crosses, which is 12 miles above Zanesville, third to feed a canal that is in progress from Zanesville to Marietta and also to supply the extensive flouring establishments. This canal is dug out of very near a solid freestone rock. It is from 10 to 12 ft. thick. This stone is, after being blown, taken and thrown into the dam, a description of which will be found in another part of this journal. This canal is for steam boat navigation. The town of Zanesville contains something like 8000 inhabitants.

At half past 9 we started. We passed by where there had been stone coal[43] dug in a number of places. This day's travel has brought us through Putnam, Zanesville, **Norwich.** Here I will name another little anecdote, an old lady came out to receive the toll which was 31½ cents. I gave her 37½ cents pay, the change coming to me was 6 cents. The old sinner looked at the quarter and said their was no pillars on it, I contended that there was and that they were plain, but she persisted in her own way and finally went and got her specks and looked at it and exclaimed, Law, it's an old fashioned one, well, I guess it's a quarter, ain't it old man? (handing it to the old fellow himself who came out goring his eyes with his knuckles). Yes, it's a quarter, and the old lady gave me my phip[44] and we put out from Norwich through **Concord, Cambridge** and **Washington.**

Figure 19. The old Muskingum County Courthouse, as it appeared when Henry visited Zanesville.

A phip, or fip, (from "fippenny") was worth one sixteenth of a dollar, or 6¼ cents.

Until the mid-19th century, people did not know microorganisms could invade the body and cause disease. Disease prevention through simple hygiene was unheard-of.

Louis Pasteur discovered that bacteria could change alcohol to vinegar. Heating the alcohol enough to kill the bacteria, but not enough to kill the yeast used in the brewing process, became known as pasteurization. Pasteur's connection between microorganisms and food spoilage in 1857 also established a link between microorganisms and disease.

In 1876, Robert Koch, a German physicist, proved that the bacterium *Bacillus anthracis* was the cause of anthrax in sheep and cattle.

Henry frequently mentioned family members' illnesses during their journey. Most likely, they were ill from drinking tainted water or eating spoiled food.

This is the most hilly country ever I traveled.[45] The road winds in almost every direction and some parts of it is very steep yet smooth. About a mile east of Washington we called and put up for the night.[46] We passed 5 gates today and our bill for breakfast was $1.50, horse feed for noon 25 cents. Maria has the headache some this evening.

Wednesday morning, 29th clear and cool, in very good health except myself. I feel very sick at my stomach, vomited twice before we started and once after.[47] Our bill for supper, lodging and horse feed was $2.00. Started on the road at sunrise and I was sick for about 5 or 6 miles so that I could not sit up. We passed by where they were manufacturing salt, but I was so sick that we did not stop to examine any of the works. We stopped at **William Armstrong's**[48] tavern and called for our breakfast. I feel at this time a considerable better, 8 o'clock. The water through this hilly country is very sulphery so that the horses nor ourselves can scarcely drink it. After we paid our bill which was $1.18¾ cents, Maria and myself are both troubled with sick stomachs. At a quarter before 1 we stopped and fed. I feel very feeble as yet, and so does Maria.

We have traveled this forenoon through a most scandalous hilly country. The road in one place tacked and right in the turn of the road on the upper side was a spring of running water where we gave our horses some and then went on climbing up the hill, which looked like the highest pinnacle. We have passed through **Middletown, Elizabethtown, Fairview, Hendrysburg,** and **Morristown.** Hendrysburg appears to be a place of some considerable business. There is a stream grist mill of some considerable magnitude and a coal bak[49] within 200 yards of the mill. The soil of this part of the country is thin but it looks as though the people lived at home by the quantity of wheat[50] and oats there appears stacked on the farms. We have come now to where it is not so hilly. Fruit appears to be more plentiful and corn is short but is well cared for. We have passed by two toll gates this forenoon. About quarter after 2 we got ready for a start. Maria still feels a little sick.

We passed through **Louisville, Richland, St. Clairsville, Bridgeport** and **Wheeling** to Virginia.[51] We ferried the west side of the island and there they charged 25 cents, then the east side where they charged 37½ cents. We then drove up in town and put up at **Mr. Beymer's**[52] hotel, where we had an excellent supper. This afternoon's travel caps the climax, of all hills that we have traveled since leaving home, and a road as crooked as a black snake.

The most fearsome and terrific rocks rising to the height of from 40 or 50 ft. perpendicular on the right, while on the left there appeared a gulch that if a carriage would run off must hurry the rider into destruction in a twinkling. There were some places that appeared to be near 1000 ft. deep. This was on the west side of Wheeling Creek in Ohio. This road went down hill for better than a mile at an angle of something like 4 or 5 degrees. Then after we got down this hill and crossed the creek we had a tolerable level road til we got into Wheeling.

This country although hilly is great agricultural country.[53] Corn is good and an abundance of wheat and almost every farm has a fountain pump. We have found some good water today that is not sulphery. Evening. We all of us appear to be a little dauney,[54] probably from the change of water that we have been used to. Passed 4 gates.

Figure 20. The Sign of the Wagon tavern was owned by Captain Beymer, and was located at the corner of Main and 9th streets in Wheeling. Established around 1802, the brick tavern may have been the structure just to the right of the bridge. This daguerreotype, made in 1852, is believed to be the oldest existing picture of Wheeling.

Most likely Henry meant "donsie" which means somewhat sick, weak, or lacking vitality; not completely well.

Henry Rogers' Journal

Virginia and Western Pennsylvania

Thursday morning, 30th. We are some little better this morning. We got 2 new shoes on the horses and one old one reset. Bill for shoeing 62½ cents. We got our faces barbered off this morning. Fees 12½ cents each. We then after breakfast made ready for a start, our bill was $4.50. We started at 9 o'clock from Wheeling on the National Road for Washington. The town of Wheeling I am not prepared to say much about, for I felt so unwell that I made but little discoveries. But I think there is not much width to the town.

The National Road runs through the center of the place from about midway of the town's length, then front of Water Street, then Market Street, which is right against the foot of the most terrific hill so that there would be but 3 rows of buildings from the river back to where they are digging out stone coal in great abundance. We crossed over Wheeling Hill in Virginia and then to mount the hills.

We passed though **Tridelphia, West Alexandria** and **Claysville**, where we stopped to feed. Charley, one of the horses, appeared to be sick and did not eat

Figure 21. The Ohio River at Wheeling, West Virginia.

his feed. We gave him about 2 oz. of No. 6[55] with water, without much effect. He appeared to be in a great deal of distress. We then gave him a ½ pint of whiskey with as much indigo as would lay on a cent, but he still did not eat. A stage driver looked at him and said he had a touch of bots, and said if I would let him he could help him. I told him to go at it. He turned the upper lip up and took his knife and cut this way, then rubbed as hard as he could with coarse salt and he said if we would hitch up and drive slow he would soon eat.

So accordingly, we started and drove 5 miles and stopped at the **Pennsylvania Inn** kept by **Mr. [John] Coluson,**[56] where we stayed all night. Father Hill has been very unwell all day and still feels quite feeble. He drank a little coffee at supper and we all retired to rest. This day's travel has been very much like the two preceding days with the exception of crossing the creek[57] which was so often that I did not pretend to keep account. There is no wooden structures across this creek on the National Road. While we passed through these hilly parts we were much delighted at the prospects of the farmers. We saw well cultivated fields that appeared to have yielded as luxuriant a harvest as ever rewarded the husbandman for his labor. Wheat, rye, oats almost incalculable.

We crossed over about 16 miles of the neck of Virginia and all the way to this place we have seen first rate corn and have found no scarcity of good water. The toll in Virginia is 20 cents for every 10 miles and Pennsylvania is 18¾ cents for every ten miles. They have splendid toll houses and iron gates. We passed 2 gates today. Our bill at Claysville was 31½ cents.

Friday morning 31st. Father is much better this morning. We got up quite early and made ready for a start. Our bill for supper, a bushel of oats, lodging, etc. $2.12½. Our horse is in good spirits and able for his allowance. We drove til about 8 o'clock and then stopped at the **Upland House** kept by **Mr. [Samuel] Hughes**[58] and called for our breakfast. This house is between Washington and

> "Number 6" consisted of ground chili pepper and myrrh steeped in ethanol. It was a popular herbal remedy in the 19th century, used to treat rheumatic and circulatory problems, as well as stomach upset. Indigo was used as a purgative.

Hillsborough on the most elevated part of the country. He keeps a first rate country house and is very accommodating and reasonable in charges. After partaking of the luxuries of the old man's table we paid our bill and departed, $1.25.

We have passed through **Washington, Hillsborough, Bealleville, Centreville, West** and **East Brownsville**. Washington is a considerable of a town appearing to be a place of business. We called to see a Mr. Yeoman and after delivering our message to him from his brother-in-law [David Anderson] we started.

Our horses being twice sick had reduced our stock of No. 6, so we thought proper to replenish our stock. After some inquiry I found a **Dr. McClure**[59] who kept a small shop opposite the college edifice[60] where I obtained a ½ pint for which I paid 37½ cents and went on back to the wagon, and got a few apples off a boy that had brought them into to town to sell.

We passed this day over some very poor land. The corn is very poor but the woods are equal to some of our Ohio crops and look as though neither had been tended very well. We got on a dividing ridge about the Upland House and continued on it for about 9 miles. To explain the situation of the country would be a repetition of a preceding part of the Journal, with one exception, that is, the situation of the country is higher.

About 4 in the afternoon we came in sight of the Monongahela River. There are some very lofty hills overlooking the town of Brownsville. We crossed the river on the bridge and our toll was 25 cents.[61] We then went on the first street and turned to the left and crossed an old narrow bridge[62] that looked as though it would scarcely bear its own weight. They are building another right above it, which is splendid. We then went on up the street along side a long protection wall that overlooked the wall. This wall is in some places 20 ft. high. The town of Brownsville is very irregularly built. The streets are so narrow that there is hardly room for a lone horse and cart to turn around without going to cross streets. And is very black.

Dr. Robert McClure occupied the lots and houses on Belle Street, across from the College, from about 1830.

Washington and Jefferson College was formed by the merging of what were originally two separate institutions, Washington College and Jefferson College. Both schools were established by Presbyterian ministers anxious to bring higher education to the area west of the Alleghenies. Decreased enrollment during the Civil War prompted the colleges to merge in 1865.

Dunlap's Creek Bridge was the first cast-iron bridge in America. It was constructed 1836–1839. Senator Henry Clay, a champion of the National Road, was "dumped into the bed of Dunlap's Creek" when his carriage overturned. Clay reportedly "gathered himself up with the remark that Clay and mud should not be mixed in that place again." Upon his return to Washington, DC, he initiated an order for an iron bridge, "carrying the road high above the stream."

Henry's Journal — Virginia and Western Pennsylvania

Figure 22. Washington & Jefferson College as it appeared ca. 1900. Old Gym, at left, was built in 1893. Old Main, at right, was built 1834–1836, and underwent major renovations 1847–1850 and again in 1875 at which time the twin towers were added to the original structure.

Figure 23. Dunlaps Creek Bridge in Brownsville, Pennsylvania.

Figure 24. Searight's Tollhouse, near Uniontown, Pennsylvania. William Searight was a Commissioner for Public Works and left the management of his tavern to others.

We then proceeded up the hill and soon came in sight of the blue ridge stretching to the right and the left almost as far as the eye could reach. We have passed through three gates today. We put up for the night at the tavern house of **Mathias Fry**,[63] 6 miles west of **Uniontown**, where we were comfortably entertained. About midnight there came up a shower and thundered and lightninged quite hard. At this place we were disturbed some, about the time of the shower, by some fellows that took shelter under the porch, where they hollered and sung like madmen.

Saturday morning Sept. 1, 1838. Cloudy and cool. Maria is so sick again this morning so that we concluded to start. We started from Fry's at half past 5 and got into **Monroe Village**[64] at half past 7. This town is right at the foot of **Laurel Hill**. We passed through Uniontown at a quarter past 7. In the village we stopped and called for our breakfast at the tavern of **G. D. Hair**.[65] At this place our breakfast was not what we had the evening before, by some odds. After breakfast we paid our bill which was $1.18¾ cents and started on our journey up the south side of the Laurel Hill.[66]

This hill is the one from which a great number of mill stones were taken and carried to the state of Ohio. But of all the hills that I ever went over this is the cap sheaf. The road winds up the hill at a grade of not over 3½ or 4 degrees, which makes the descent so gradual one would hardly know they were climbing a mountain were he not to cast his eyes above and below and view with astonishment the stupendous height on the left, towering almost to the clouds while on the right almost perpendicular descending to the distance of some hundreds of feet and the rocks hanging (one could think) by the eyelids just ready to fall on the passing traveler, yet there is something grand exposed to the sight.

After reaching the summit of this hill, look back and you can see the hills and all the adjoining country east of Brownsville and from the hill after leaving

Figure 25. These granite millstones, on display at Stanton's Mill near Garrettsville, Maryland, are cut in the wagon wheel pattern.

Brownsville you can see in the Blue Ridge a part of a turnpike road which looks off a while east and it is from this spot when you ascend to it that you have the most extensive prospect going up this hill. I saw the first huckleberry bushes that I ever saw. I went out in search of some berries but found none.

We then proceeded up the hill till we came to where there was a protection wall curved about in a circle of 100 ft. by 40 ft. high. Then came the pines reaching their tops to the very clouds. This hill is covered with laurel, sweet briar, huckleberry and hosts of other strange weeds to me. Chestnut trees in abundance. The rocks lay so thick over the ground that in most places a man may travel for some distance over them without touching the ground. There is about midway of the mountains a spring which is fixed for the convenience of watering horses.[67] I think I would like to spend a day or two in these mountains with a gun so that if anything was to disturb me I could bring it to a settlement in a twinkling for it is very snakish about these parts and looks like the habitations of satyrs and foul spirits or ghosts.

We had, from the foot of the hill on the east side, a long stretch of straight road running south east. There is between the Laurel Hill and the mountains some tolerably good farms for hay. Oats they have not took up yet, and one field we saw was green corn. There is none worth naming. Buckwheat is the best we have seen anywhere in our travel. We stopped to feed about 1 o'clock where we found some very large hemlock trees. After feeding we started.

We have come this day through the towns of **Uniontown, Monroe, Smythfield** and **Petersburgh**. Uniontown lies 2 miles west of Laurel Hill and is considerable of a business place being the county seat of Union County. Smythfield is on the waters of the **Yoghiogeny River** that runs down through the mountains 20 miles east of Uniontown. Petersburgh is 2 miles and a half west of the boundary line between Pennsylvania and Maryland and has every appearance of being a scandalous cold place.

Along between Petersburgh and **Frostburgh** we saw a number of tobacco houses[68] and several fields where the deadened chestnut trees were very thick all over the field. We passed 3 gates today[69] and the last one was 2 miles from the Maryland line. Maria has been very sick all this day until evening. She got some better so that she eat some supper. We stopped for the night at the tavern house of **Mr. Stoddard**[70] in Allegeny County State of Maryland, on the highest piece of ground between Baltimore and Wheeling.[71]

The wind whistles through the trees like November and feels like it, too. The fire feels this evening as though we would like to change our thin clothes for some a little thicker. What a contrast between the last night in August and the first night of September. The former so warm that we could not sleep and the latter so cold that a warming pan was almost wanted.

Figure 26. The Addison (Petersburgh) tollhouse is owned by the Great Crossings Chapter of the Daughters of the American Revolution.

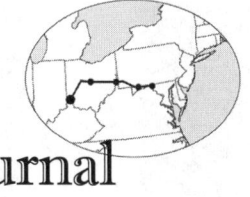

Henry Rogers' Journal

5

Maryland

    Sunday morning September 2. Cloudy and cold. We all seem to be in tolerably fair spirits and health. The stages come in this morning and the passengers complain of the cold a little. We have regulated our apparel to suit the climate and feel much better. We called for our breakfast before we started, about half past 6. We got ready, paid our bill for supper, lodging a bushel and a half of oats and horses to hay all night, breakfast, etc. $3.87½. This house has good accommodations.

    We drove on over mountains and through valley past some most delightful groves of large and small hemlock trees. We crossed over a stone culvert this forenoon that was raised on base walls about 80 ft. high and 50 ft. span. The stone that the arch was turned with were hewed freestone.[72]

    The morning was very cold for the season. We felt as if our fur caps would feel comfortable. We stopped a number of times for huckleberries but without much success. At length we came up with a boy that said there were stacks of them up on the Meadow Mountain[73] and he was going up there. Distance, a mile. We stopped on the Meadow Mountain and gathered some berries, but the stacks that the boy told of was not there.

Figure 27. The Casselman Bridge in Grantsville, Maryland, was the largest single-arch bridge in the United States at the time of its construction in 1813.

Figure 28. The National Road west of Frostburg, Maryland.

Figure 29. The bridge at the Narrows at Wills Creek was built in 1836.

The first white pines we came to was 12 miles west of Frostburg and continued on more or less till we came to Frostburg. One mile east of the town we stopped to feed where there was an extensive fountain pump. After feeding we started first on one mountain then in a valley until we came to where the National Road has been altered and it now goes on a level or nearly so. This afternoon has furnished us with a great many curiosities. Within 3 miles of **Cumberland** we came in sight of 2 mountains which is ad captandum,[74] or the match not to be found. These mountains are not of rocks but of one rock rising to the height of 5 or 600 ft. above the level of the road, it running right at the foot and the rock rising almost perpendicular above.[75] There is a creek running in between these two monsters called the **Wills Creek** that empties into the Potomac at Cumberland. In short it seems as though nature had exhausted all her resources in forming these gigantic walls in the most deformed manner possible.[76] The passenger is lost in admiration, surprise and wonder.

After leaving this place of rocks, we came to a most splendid bridge made across Wills Creek of very superior limestone with 2 arches and iron railing. Then we took the **Baltimore Road** and begun to climb the hills and passed through some handsome groves of yellow pine of all sizes from 20 inches and under. We saw directly after going over the first mountain large clouds of smoke which on enquiring found out to be a fire in the mountain. We called at a public house for entertainment and they had no horse feed. Then another and ditto. Then on about 2 miles further we found a place and put up for the night at the tavern about 8 o' clock. This place is rather savage. We got supper and went to bed.[77]

Monday morning, September 3. Clear and cold. After paying the bill, $2.25, we started. Our horses seem to be very stiff and sore and can scarcely travel. I started and walked on before and came to a town called **Flintstone**. This town is well named for there is a creek running through the town that has nothing but round flint stone in it. After leaving town I came to a small grist and saw mill on the same stream.[78] We then began to climb another mountain winding round the north side, for 3 miles up hill, till at length we came to the backbone (as I thought) of the world. We could see over a vast extent of country. This I learned was **Polish Mountain**[79] and had a house on the top.

We called at the **tavern** of **Philip Fletcher**[80] and called for our breakfast. I saw a considerable frost this morning in walking from the Fletcher's. This is a good house and is situated on the east side of Polish Mountain, 23½ miles west of Hancock and 16 miles east of Cumberland. Then there is another good house between Town Hill and Sideling Hill. This at this time is a stage house and is 9 miles from Fletcher's.[81] At this place we stopped and fed. After breakfast we paid our bill $1.25 and started. And 12½ cents for setting a shoe on Charley. He has been very stiff all day so that we have not drove off a walk all day.

We have passed 3 gates of 10 miles and one half gate. The toll on this road is 25 cents for every 10 miles. The top of Sideling Hill[82] commands the greatest prospect of any other mountain we have crossed. East, west, or south you can see over a vast extent of country. I think from the top of Laurel Hill to this place is the poorest corn that I ever saw. Some places it is not more than 2 ft., from that to 5 ft. high, and no corn or even a nubbin to be seen. Many have turned their cattle in. The frost has now nipped it and they are obliged to cut it up for fodder.

They have had no rain on the mountains for about 2 months to do any good to the vegetation. Oats, there is hardly any. And what there is is not worth gathering for the grain. We saw today a man cradling where the straw was not more than 18 or 20 inches high. We called at the tavern house of **Mr. [Jacob] Brosious**[83] miles west of Hancock and 37 miles west of Cumberland where we put up for the night and called for our supper. We traveled about 27 miles.

Figure 30. Part of the National Road on the west side of Sideling Hill, west of Hancock, Maryland.

Henry's Journal — Maryland

Tuesday morning Sept. 4. Clear, cold and frost. All well this morning and the horses a considerable better. Started quite early after paying our bill, $2.60. We passed through **Hancock** that lies on the Potomac River about 7 in the morning, and stopped for breakfast at the **Widow Bevins,** 3 miles east of Hancock.[84] After breakfast we paid our bill, $1.25, and started. We followed the river for 7 miles then the road leaves the river just at a toll gate. **The Chesapeake and Ohio Canal** runs between the road and the river as we followed it. Mrs. Bevins' is a house of good accommodations that can be recommended to travelers. **Blair's Tavern** west of the **Indian Spring** does not look very nice. Keep away from it at any rate. The **Indian Spring House** has every appearance of being a first rate house.[85]

After leaving the river we proceeded to climb over some small hills until we came to the Indian Spring, where we tried to get our tyers cut, but the blacksmith said he had too much to do, and another thing, he said he was drunk. We went on about ¾ of a mile further to another shop to the same effect as before except the man was not drunk. Here is another tavern quite comely in appearance. At this place there was water running along a long train of small troughs that were fastened on forks about as high as the fence, appearing to be brought down the hill about 70 or 80 yards distant. I got out of the wagon and took the cup, saying I would get some from the fountain, but when I got to it, it was not there. Then I followed the train of troughs through the woods for about 50 or 60 rods until it began to go up the mountain and I could see, as I thought, about 80 rods further up the mountain where the train still continued. This water is for the convenience of wagoners and travelers that call at this tavern.

We then went over a considerable of a mountain and then came in sight of the town called **Clear Spring**. Here we got out tyers cut and bill $1.25. There are some good taverns in this place. About half past 3 we went out of this place for

Mrs. Bevins' (or Bevans') house may have been a house of good accommodations in 1838, but a November, 1879, *Harper's New Monthly Magazine* article entitled "The Old National Pike" described Mrs. Bevans' house quite differently.

"Between Hancock and Cumberland the road is almost deserted, and there is no tavern in over forty miles. We were told that we might find accommodations for the night at 'Mrs. Bevans's,' and as the day sped... Mrs. Bevans became a tremendous object of interest to us. Near sundown... it was evident that our team was unfit to go much farther, but no habitation was in sight, although from time to time we saw an abandoned toll-house or tavern, and once we met a freckled boy, who said it was about five miles to 'Mrs. Bevans's.' We continued on for over six miles, and then we met a freckled and angular man. We labored over another mountain and down a rocky road... At the foot, in a hollow, was a splendid old tavern, unroofed, moss-grown, windowless, and doorless. This was 'Mrs. Bevans's' in the past, and at one side of it, in contrast with its massive masonry, was a small cabin of two rooms, with some six or seven unappetizing children about the door; this was the 'Mrs. Bevans's' of the present. It was out of the question; the children took the edge off our hunger, and we urged the horses farther on, being informed that we would find a farm-house on the summit of the next mountain."

41

Fips, Bots, Doggeries, and More

Figure 31. The Conococheague Creek Aqueduct was built in 1834, at the Chesapeake and Ohio Canal, near Williamsport, Maryland.

Figure 33. Lock 44, Chesapeake and Ohio Canal near Williamsport, Maryland.

Figure 32. Wilson's Bridge, built 1817–1819, bore traffic on the National Road for nearly 80 years. It has been closed to traffic since 1972.

Figure 34. Tollhouse at Cumberland, Maryland.

Hagerstown. We passed over a creek between Clear Spring and Hagerstown where there is an extension stone bridge turned in three arches.[86] There is a mill just above the bridge on the east side.[87] This is about 8 miles from Hagerstown. From there on to Hagerstown and put up at the **Rising Sun,** kept by **Frech & Hershner**.[88] This house I did not like for there appeared to be too many topers about.

    We have passed some handsome improvements in this days travel and very extensive stockyards. The farmers seem to be preparing very largely for seeding. This is the most stony and rocky of any country I have traveled through for the people to pretend to farm on so large a scale as they do here. We got through the pine timber before we got to Clear Spring, but we passed some cedar on the aforesaid creek. We passed gates half and gates whole, to the amount of $1 toll. We went out in the evening and got our faces barbered off for 6½ cents each.

Henry Rogers' Journal

Eastern Pennsylvania

Wednesday morning the 5th. Clear and pleasant and all well. We prepared for making a start after paying our bill, $2.00. We left Hagerstown for **Leitersburg,** 6 miles. As we passed the Hagerstown market we bought some peaches and blue plums. Arrived in L-burg about 7 and called at the tavern of **Mr. [John] Lahm**[89] for breakfast and horse feed. After breakfast paid our bill $1.25 and put out for the South Mountain over the meanest and roughest road we have traveled and a part of this is turnpike and a gate about halfway over where we paid 12½ cents toll. We then passed through a village called **Fairfield,** from thence to **Gettysburg**, a distance from Hagerstown of 32 miles. From thence to the sign of the **Cross Keys,**[90] kept by a Dutchman where we put up for the night.

This days travels have been through a strange part of the country. The land generally looks rich but has rocks of the most gigantic size laying just beneath the surface with their edges up and in many places rising up to the height of 6 inches to 2 feet. I can compare them to nothing else at a distance but a newly cleared field where the timber is very thick on the ground and very large. We stopped at 1 o'clock at the Tavern of **J. Weigle**[91] and fed. Fairfield is 8 miles west of Gettysburg

Figure 35. This field near Antietam, Maryland, looked just as Henry described the landscape when he traveled through the area.

and 4 miles west of the foot of the South Mountain. The dust has been the worst today that is has been since we have been on the road. Corn continues to be poor. Peaches and apples are plenty, but small. This house is 3 miles from Gettysburg on the road to York.

Thursday morning, 6th. Clear and pleasant. We rose about 4 o'clock this morning and prepared for an early start, being well all but tired of traveling. After paying our bill of $2.12½ we left at 5 o'clock. We passed through **New Oxford** where we watered the horses. From thence to **Abbotstown** where we called at the tavern of **James Fink**[92] for our breakfast and horsefeed. After paying the bill $1.31½, we left for **York**, where we arrived at quarter past 1 and got our horses fed at the **Golden Lamb** kept by **Peter Wilt**.[93]

From thence to **Columbia** through 2 miles to the tavern kept by **Joshua Taylor**.[94] While we were in York Father Hill and myself went down to the landing of the railroad cars. They come in at 12 and go out at 2:00. We got there about the time they were going to start. They started off like as though the old scratch[95] had sent them. Returned, paid the bill, 25 cents, and started at half past 2. The next place we came to was **Wrightsville**, at the west end of the bridge across the Susquehannah River.[96] This bridge is about a mile in length and the railroad cars sometimes pass over to Wrightsville with horse power. York is the handsomest town I have saw since I left Ohio. It contains something like 4500 inhabitants. Its principal streets run east and west. It also has some cross streets, all of which is wide, airy and pleasant. Columbia I cannot say much about, as it was just night when we passed through but as far as I was able to discover it is a business place. A railroad from Philadelphia which unites the **Pennsylvania Canal** and several stage lines which make arrivals and departures very speedy and commercial intercourse, etc.

There are 2 reservoirs east of the town that are fed from springs that supply the place with water. They are building a dam across the river to feed a canal that

Figure 36. The western entrance to York, Pennsylvania, about 1843.

"Old Scratch" is slang for the Devil.

The first covered bridge at Columbia, constructed in 1812, was the longest covered bridge in the world at the time. That bridge was destroyed by ice and high water in 1832. The second bridge, completed in 1834, was more than a mile long, with 27 stone piers, a carriageway, separate walkway, and two towpaths for canal traffic crossing the river. It was also the longest covered bridge in the world.

This second bridge was burned by Union troops the week before the battle of Gettysburg, to stall approaching Confederate troops.

Figure 37. Covered bridge over the Susquehanna River, Columbia, Pennsylvania.

Figure 38. North Queen Street in Lancaster, Pennsylvania.

is to run from Columbia to Baltimore[97] then to be towed across the river on a path constructed on the piers from the lower side of the bridge and then intersect the Pennsylvania Canal in the east side of the river. There were a number of cars on the railroad in Columbia but none in operation. This days travel has been through the handsomest and best improved country east of the mountain.[98] The farms are in the very best possible order. Barns are the most splendid buildings that are in this country. Many I suppose to be 80 or 100 feet in length, built of brick and stone, and some of timber, above the base, with dormer windows ornamented like a mansion house. In short it looks like the most fertile and agricultural region I have noticed.

Friday morning September 7th. Clear and pleasant. All well and in tolerably good spirits. Got up at half past 4 and after paying our bill, $2.50, started for **Lancaster**. There we arrived about half past 7 and called for our breakfast and horses feed at the **Sign of the Leopard**[99] kept by **J. H. Duchman**.[100] After paying our bill, $1.50, we left Lancaster and took the road to **New Holland**. We passed through New Holland about half past 1 and about half past 2 we stopped at the **tavern** of **Henry Yuntz**[101] where we fed our horses. At a quarter before 3 we started, passing through **Churchtown, Morgantown** and from thence to the tavern of **David Hasta,**[102] a first rate old Jacksonian where we put up for the night.

Lancaster is the largest town we have passed through. It is a considerable of a mercantile place. The railroad running from Philadelphia to it, passenger trains twice a day and the burthen trains[103] arriving and departing almost every hour. When we left the town, first thing that attracted our notice was the splendid reservoir[104] that supplies the town with water forced by water-power from the Conestoga River up to it. This reservoir is placed upon the highest ground and is made by throwing the earth up in the shape or a mound

4 square to the height of 15 ft. This is hollowed to the center at an angle of about 8 degrees and that paved with brick on edge. This reservoir contains about an acre of ground. On the top of it was a paled fence[105] four feet high with a beautiful graveled walk around the outside. The path is sufficiently wide for two persons to stand side by side. The outside of the reservoir is most elegantly sodded from top to bottom. The outside is about 45 degrees. The whole is fenced in with a pale fence including about 2½ acres of ground which they are now ornamenting with shrubbery of various kinds. Up on the east and west sides there are two flights of steps for the purpose of getting up to the top of the reservoir. The water is remarkably clear. Upon the whole it is a splendid place.

From thence to the bridge that crossed the Conestoga. This is made of stone entire and has 9 arches. Whole length about 450 feet. The next was a train of cars going from Lancaster to Philadelphia. The town of New Holland is about a mile in length, and has the appearance of being an old place. It looks quite romantic in consequence of low building and the fronts handsomely shaded with white mulberry and other handsome shade trees. Churchtown is very small with 2 or 3 public houses. Morgantown looks as though it was about to give up the ghost.

This days travel has been through what is called the Conestoga Valley. This is a beautiful part of the country. The best looking farms, farmhouses and all other buildings necessary to make a country desirable.[109] Almost every farmhouse has a spring of never failing water running as clear as crystal. Mills of elegant appearance are very numerous, propelled by water from those springs. The corn and pasturage assume a little better prospect than it has for a day or two back. Apples are not so plenty as they have been, but peaches are abundant wherever there are trees that are thrifty. We passed today two 37½ cent gates, one 4 cent gate just as we stopped. This has been the roughest turnpike we have traveled. The past two days have been very warm.

Figure 39. Witmer's Bridge, Lancaster, Pennsylvania.

Henry Rogers' Journal

7

Trenton and Hunterdon County

Saturday morning Sept. 8. Clear and pleasant, all well and ready for our allowance. Got up at quarter past 4 and made ready for a start. After paying the bill $1.25 we started for Pawlings Bridge on what is called the Ridge Road. The road is very dusty and we passed by where there was a Methodist camp meeting near a place called **Coventry**.

At a quarter past 9 we stopped at the **Sign of the 7 Stars**[107] kept by **George Kristman**[108] and called for our breakfast and horse feed. This man is also a Jacksonian and a Dutchman and keeps a first rate house. After breakfast we paid our bill $1.25 and started on for Pawlings Bridge on the Schuylkill River. This is a toll bridge, 12½ cents. From hence to **Norristown** and thence to the **Sign of the Broad Axe Tavern**[109] 6 miles from Norristown kept by **Mrs. [Ann] Acuff**.[110] There we put up for the night. Norristown lays on the Schuylkill River 16 miles above Philadelphia. There is slack water navigation up as far as Reading.[111] There is also a railroad now in operation from Philadelphia through Norristown to Reading. This has been in operation about 3 weeks. The town is beautifully situated on the river and presents a lively and healthy appearance.

Figure 40. On the canal at Norristown, Pennsylvania.

Figure 42. The Seven Stars Tavern near Phoenixville in East Vincent Township, Pennsylvania. The Seven Stars' website lists George Christman as one of the former owners of the tavern, just as Henry recorded in his journal.

Figure 41. Broad Axe Tavern in Ambler, Whitpain Township, Pennsylvania, was completely renovated in 2009, and is now open as a restaurant.

Figure 43. Revolutionary Soldiers Cemetery, East Vincent Township, Pennsylvania.

This days travel has been quite interesting. The road is called the Ridge Road and so it was on a ridge from morning until almost noon where we crossed the stream called **French Creek** and so on until we crossed the Schuylkill. In the fore part of the day we had tolerably rough road to travel over, but after crossing the aforesaid streams our road was excellent except so very dusty. This forenoon we passed by where there were 22 Revolutionary Soldiers buried on a small piece of ground purported to have been owned by a man by the name of Henry Hipple who preserved it untilled from 1777 until the fall of 1831, when the Chester County Battalion of Volunteers declared their intention of having the ground enclosed and a monument erected to their memory so that the present and future generations yet unborn might see where and under what circumstances those true and patriotic Sons of Liberty and Independence perished.[112]

It was this Battalion, aided by the patriotic yeomanry of the country, that Foundation of the excellent stone wall which now encloses the spot in which the remains of those long forgotten worthies were interred. Between 1831 and 1833 the ground was enclosed and a plain yet large marble monument erected. It was on the 25th day of October 1833, in the presence of a large crowd of people, that the monument was raised and dedicated. Those 22 true Sons of Columbia were lodged in the **Dutch Reform Church**[113] in the sight of the Valley Forge, which was then occupied as a hospital for the American Army. There they were, far from their homes, uncomforted by friends and no smooth soft hand of affection to console them in their dying moments.

Sunday morning Sept. 9. All well except Mother. She is complaining of headache and cold in the head. We concluded to take breakfast before we started out and accordingly after breakfast we paid our bill $3.12½ and started out at a quarter before 7 for **Newton**. At half past 12 we stopped at the **Sign of the**

Figure 44. The Spread Eagle Tavern, Richboro, Pennyslvania, was known as the Sign of the Bear when Henry stopped there. The mansard roof and gallery porch were added in the 1890s.

Bear[114] and fed our horses. After paying the bill, 25 cents, we started. This house is 4 miles from Newton, 9 miles from **Yardleyville**, and 21 miles from Philadelphia. We passed through Yardleyville, crossed the bridge[115] at that place and went out to **John Hendrickson's**[116] and he and his wife being gone from home, we proceeded to **Wm. Hendrickson's**,[117] where we joyfully were received. In the evening **Asher Hill**[118] and John Hendrickson and his son **William**[119] came to see us. After spending some time in agreeable and social intercourse with one another, they dispersed.

This days travel has been very tedious in consequence of roads. We missed our way in the morning and got about 2 miles out of the way. The road is very crooked so that is was with difficulty we made much speed, having to make frequent enquiries. We at length got on the top of the hill that overlooks the Delaware River and there we had a full view of the old Jersey shore looking as blue as the Allegheny Mountains.

Last evening we perceived that our unseemly protuberances of the chin becoming somewhat disgusting, we therefore resolved to call for some tools in order to effect a removal. According, an elderly gentleman who was no more than a boarder [at the Broad Axe Tavern] furnished us with the necessary implements for the purpose, while a kind of groom that was in attendance about the house furnished us with warm water to wash and a towel to dry our faces. With all these things being ready Father Hill first made an attempt to shave. After some of the most severe, harrowing and savage looks, [his] wry face bespoke that the tool was a kind of harrow tooth.

I next took up the implement and began to strap it, in order that I might effect my purpose with as much ease as possible but it was all in vain. I commenced and must admit here that another such a tour I never had. For every stroke of the razor (or harrow tooth as it ought to be called) it seemed to me as though

Fips, Bots, Doggeries, and More

> Paper mills of Henry's era ground up cotton and linen rags to make paper pulp. This had been essentially the only method of making paper in the Western world from the 16th Century until the wood pulp method was perfected in the 1860s.

hide and hair was coming. It is now Monday and my face is sore from having so much of the beard pulled out by the roots. I concluded the next time I [must] shave, or rather pull out my beard, with such a tool, I'll let it alone.

Monday morning, Sept. 10, 1838. Mother Hill has the sick headache very bad. The rest of us are all in tolerably good health. We found that by some means or other the keys of our trunks got left where we stayed Saturday night and as our trunks were locked we were obliged to take one trunk and go down to **Trenton** to a locksmith and get a new key. While I was there I went and took a squint at the sloops lying in the basin. After getting our job accomplished, I went in company with **Mr. R. Hunt**[120] to see **Israel Hendrickson,**[121] where I stayed until after dark. Then he went with me to Wm. Hendrickson's.

Tuesday morning 11th. Looks very much like rain. All reasonably well, except Mother. She is considerable better. We started this morning to R. Hunt's [in Ewing Township] where we tarried and took dinner. After dinner Father Hill and myself went with Israel Hendrickson and son **Wm**.[122] down to Trenton. While there we visited the paper mill,[123] and 2 or 3 elegant saw mills.[124] Then to the flour and oil mills of **Mr. Moore**.[125] All of which are propelled by water taken out of the Delaware River four miles above Trenton. At 5 o'clock we left town and returned to Hunt's then proceeded to I. Hendrickson's, where we made our calculations to stay all night. While at Mr. Hunt's we saw **[Benjamin] Stout Hill**[126] passing by and called to him. He halted a few minutes and then put out going to Trenton from thence to Philadelphia to buy plaster.

Wednesday morning 12th. Mother has a very bad cold, hoarse and sick headache. Began to rain sometime in the night and still keeps on with high winds. About 5 in the evening we left for Asher Hill's. About 2 miles distant we stopped and delivered a letter to Mrs. Hendrickson. We got to Mr. Hill's in the midst of the heavy rain. About 8 o'clock in the evening the wind began to blow very hard with

Henry's Journal — Trenton and Hunterdon County

increased torrents of rain which continued the principal part of the night. John Hendrickson got weather bound and was obliged to stay the night. There has been more or less rain all day.

Thursday morning 13th. We are all of us in tolerably good health. It is clear this morning with high winds. We left Mr. Hill's about 11 o'clock and went to John Hendrickson's, about 5 o'clock **David Hill**,[127] his wife and wife's mother came down on their way to Trenton. After supper they started together with Father and Mother Hill for Wm. Hendrickson's and Maria and myself stayed with Israel Hendrickson all night.

Friday morning 14th. We went with I. Hendrickson to Wm. Hendrickson's and found them all well. We all went with David Hill, his wife and his wife's mother down to Trenton. There they traded some and went back to Wm. H's, took supper and went on home [back to Ewing]. There is nothing new of any note occurred today.

Saturday morning 15th. We are all in good health and making preparations to go up the country, the women having washed their clothes last evening. Towards the evening we got ready and started for Mr. [Benjamin] Stout Hill's where we arrived about sunset and found them all well. Mr. Hill has gone to a Democratic meeting but we were very agreeably entertained by his **wife**,[128] **Jane**[129] and **Juliet Ann**[130] his daughters, and David his son.

Sunday morning 16th. We are all well. Clear and cold winds. We went to the Baptist Church at Hopewell[131] and heard a sermon delivered by **J. Boggs.**[132] After which we returned to Mr. Hill's, took dinner and went again at 4 o'clock to the Union School House. There we had another discourse from the aforesaid minister.

Monday morning 17th. All well this morning, cloudy and cool and windy. After breakfast we started for **David Hill's**,[133] where we arrived at about half past 12 and found them all in good health. We went the road that goes through **New**

Figure 45. The Baptist Meeting House, Hopewell, New Jersey, was built in 1747 on a parcel of land donated by John Hart, a signer of the Declaration of Independence.

Reverend John Boggs was pastor at Hopewell Baptist Church from 1809 until his death in 1846. A Reverend Boggs is listed as officiate at a number of marriages in Hunterdon County, New Jersey, including Benjamin Stout Hill and Margaret Vandike's marriage.

Market.[134] The face of the country through this part is quite different from that in the vicinity of Trenton. That is, the latter being a gravelly or rather a sandy sort of soil. It appears to be covered with small flint stones and is naturally very thin poor land and quite level.[135] That of the former is quite mountainous and there appears to be a kind of red shell rock lying just beneath the surface and of which the fields seem to be covered, broken into small pieces. The earth appears to have the same color of the rocks.[136]

David Hill, Father Hill and myself went down to Clover Hill and **Squire Jacob Williamson's mill**.[137] After looking through the mill in company with Harry, the black boy, we went in to see the old lady and gentleman. After spending some time in very agreeable and social intercourse on various subjects, etc. The day being very nigh spent, we took leave of the friends and returned.

Tuesday morning 18th. All well, clear and quite warm, and pleasant. Nothing of any note occurred this day, only looking over the farm and visiting a **Mrs. Sutphen**[138] by Mr. and Mrs. Hill, Mother and Father Hill. In the evening we all went to a society or prayer meeting to the Baptist meeting house. We got back at 11 o'clock at night.

Wednesday morning 19th. All well as usual, clear and pleasant and a little cool. After breakfast Father and myself went out to look over the **Somerset** farm now owned by Mr. Sutphen but formerly to Asher Hill and came to where there were some fox grapes, the vines running over an apple tree. I ascended and threshed the tree or the vines of some of the fruit, which was very delicious and then gathered up the fruit and went up to the house. Mr. Sutphen being gone from there, we went back after dinner. We hitched our horses to D. Hill's wagon and in company with him and his wife we went to visit a **Mr. Hoagland** and his **wife**. They live on the south branch of the Raritan River. There we saw **Mrs. Schenck** and her **two daughters**, one of which was married to a **Wm. Cain**.[139] After spending the afternoon and evening in the most agreeable manner possible we returned at half past 10.

Thursday morning 20th. Clear and pleasant. All were between hawk and buzzard[140] about going back to Trenton, and finally gave up the chase and concluded to go to visit Squire J. Williamson and accordingly about 2 o'clock we went in company with D. Hill and wife, down to Williamson's. A part of the time the men spent in the mill and the remainder of the time in the house with the women. At about sunset we all sat down to tea with Mr. and Mrs. Williamson. After supper we concluded to go home. The old gentleman went on and called for Harry to go and fetch the horses. I went out and helped Harry to hitch them. We took leave of the good people and went home.

Friday morning 21st. Cloudy and drizzly a little. All well and preparing for the start. We started at 8 o'clock in the midst of a smart shower of rain for **Aaron Prawl's**,[141] passing through **Hightstown**[142] and it rained all the way until we got up to **Peter Wilson's**[143] where we stopped and took dinner. The old nigger come and took the horses and put them up in the stable and we went in the house. We stopped at Prawl's and delivered two letters and started on to Wilson's. After dinner I took a letter for **Joseph Hunt**[144] who lives in **Lambertsville** and went down on foot. I found the residence of Mr. Hunt. His wife said he had gone to Philadelphia so I delivered the letter to his wife and stepped out through town to the Hopewell Bridge and found nothing very extraordinary. I returned to Mr. Wilson's where I got about 5 o'clock. We feasted first rate on a watermelon and then got our horses and started for **Samuel Hill's**[145] where we arrived at about sunset. The boys, **Nathaniel** and **Charles**, put up the horses. Their father was gone to Philadelphy market with a load of potatoes and we did not get to see him. He has got a host of old wagons, carts, sleds, ploughs, and many other articles too tedious to mention. We were very agreeably entertained by his wife and **Hannah**

The phrase "between hawk and buzzard" conveys indeterminateness. It is defined as "between a good thing and a bad thing of the same kind" and "not quite a lady or gentleman, but not quite of the servant class".

his daughter and Nathaniel his son. This afternoon has been very pleasant. In the evening the wind began to blow very hard and continued so all night but no rain after 3 o'clock in the afternoon.

Saturday 22. All well this morning. Cloudy and blustery with signs of rain. After breakfast Father Hill, Nathaniel, and myself went round the place as far as **Mr. Stout's** where we found him, his wife and daughter all well. They live on **Mr. S. Hill's** place. After we spent a short time we returned through Mr. Hill's cornfield meadow, etc. to the house and prepared to go down to Trenton. After receiving some small presents from the girls for their cousins in the west we took leave of the family and started for Trenton, a distance of 13 miles. We passed through **Harbourton** and **Birmingham** and arrived at Trenton at half past 12. Stopped at the house of the Miss Smiths[146] where Mother and Maria were getting some dresses made.[147] They had previously made arrangements for a visit at this place on their return and there were to be in company with **Grandma Hendrickson**[148] and Eleanor their sister, now the wife of Israel Hendrickson. Father Hill and myself took the wagon and went up to Wm. and Israel Hendrickson's for the absent guests. Eleanor did not go in consequence of some work she had on hand. We then (after dinner) returned with Grandmother H. to the aforesaid place and then went to get our horses shod.

While the horses were shoeing, I went down to the canal, crossed at the lock, near the basin and went down the new railroad that is building on the bank of the canal to the depot where the cars stop and detach the locomotive and attach a pair of horses to the train, and bring them to town. At this place they wood, water and turn the cars about to suit the direction they want to go. From thence to the Pivot bridge below the depot and then back up into town to a barber shop where I went in and got the barber to shave the forepart of my

A dressmaker of this period would create a muslin pattern for each customer with a sloper, which was a lightweight cardboard template. The pattern, with a simple jewel neckline and a narrow skirt, was then used as a guide to create a more elaborate gown.

Figure 46. The canal and railroad at Trenton, New Jersey. The railroad was under construction at the time of Henry's visit.

head for which he taxed me 6½ cents. I adjusted myself and went up to the blacksmith shop and he had just finished the job, for which he taxed us 87½ cents.

We then went back to the aforesaid ladies' dwelling and were conducted upstairs among the women. We did not stay very long before we went out into town and Father got his face barbered off for 6½ cents. I looked in the post office for some letters but found none. Went back to the house and took a feed of peaches and pears. At early candle lighting we all sat down to tea. Just then Israel Hendrickson and his wife Eleanor came, sat down and took tea with us. After supper the women went out to the milliner's after their bonnets which they had taken away to get trimmed. I then left there and went in company with Israel H. to Moore's Mill where he contracted with him for his corn. Father went on with the women in the wagon to I. Hendrickson's and we came on foot where we stayed all night.

Henry Rogers' Journal

City Living

Sunday morning September 23. Windy and warm, cloudy and rainy. All in tolerably good health. After breakfast we left for Wm. Hendrickson's. John Hendrickson came down this morning and stayed til after breakfast and we all started together. We stopped at Wm. H and he went on home. We staid until after dinner and then went to I. H.'s where we staid all night. This day has been very showery and the latter part of the day has been quite blustery and cool. In the evening at suppertime Israel Hendrickson and his wife came and staid until after dark. The evening cleared off and feels like frost.

Monday morning 24th. All well this morning. Clear and quite cool but no frost of any note. After breakfast we thought of starting to Philadelphia, but John and Sarah [Hendrickson] said we should not go till after dinner for they were going to roast a pig and make some apple dumplings so of course we staid till after dinner and then put out and stopped at the Wm. H's in order to regulate some of our affairs and things. Grandmother Hendrickson has been with us from Saturday till this time 2 o'clock. Here we left her and proceeded down to Trenton. There we stopped and went in the Trenton Bank to draw $70.88 deposited there by David Anderson and certificate bought of him by Dukemenere & Martin[149] of Fletcher, O., to be paid to Williamson, Burroughs & Clark of Philadelphia for goods. After making the necessary arrangements we loaded up and started. We left Trenton at 3 o'clock and soon came to the Trenton Bridge, paid our toll 25 cents and then proceeded on.

> Isaac Dukemenere owned a store in Fletcher, Ohio. He was married to Eliza Hill's cousin, Ann Duer.

Father and Mother called a few minutes to see their cousin **Patience Jones** and **Letitia Barwis**[150] and make some enquiry about their friends in Philadelphia and where they lived. We left them and went on to **Mrs. White's**[151] residence and her son **George White** and **Rebecca** were at home. The old lady and her youngest daughter Becky living about a mile distant on the road we had come. Father and Mother went back in the wagon and brought them home with them. Maria and myself staid until they returned which was about sunset. We enjoyed a goodly satisfaction with them. Maria had a headache a little in the evening and went to bed early. About half past 10 we all went to bed and slept soundly until daylight next morning.

Tuesday morning 25th. Rose this morning in good health. A little cool and rather hazy. After breakfast we sat and talked a while and then hitched our horses and started for Philadelphia where we arrived at 2 o'clock and put up our horses at the **Sign of the White Horse**.[152] John Hendrickson was to meet us at this place. After putting our horses in the care of the hostler I walked out to see if I could see him. I met him a few doors below and went back and called for dinner. While they were preparing dinner I went to writing and John Hendrickson and Father went out. I do not know where. They returned at half hour and we sat down, ate dinner, called for our horses, paid our bill, $1.25, and started to see the **Fairmount Water Works**[153] which is on the west side of the city. After viewing the works we left about sunset and went in search of **Israel Biles**.[154] We found his residence in Moyamensing on Fitzwater Street between 9th and 10th on Morris Street. After the

Figure 47. Fairmount Water Works was the first municipal water system in the United States, designed in 1812 and built between 1819–1822.

59

Figure 48. Independence Hall, Philadelphia.

Figure 49. Market Street, Philadelphia, in the 1840s.

women got out and made themselves known John Hendrickson and myself went back to the White Horse tavern, put up the horses and called for our supper.

After supper we went out to an auction and the fellow told some tall lies about his goods. We left that and then went to Scot's Oyster Cellar, took a dose of stewed oysters and then returned to the tavern and went to bed. It began to rain a little before we got back and continued to rain all night. We saw a new thing under the sun today. It was a harrow and sled all made fast together so that when they wanted to move the harrow all they had to do was turn it over and the harrow was on the top of the sled and when they wanted to harrow turn it back again.

Wednesday morning 26th. Rose early this morning and found it to be raining, so that we could not get about with much comfort. The wind blew strong from the northeast and rained very hard, however we went out after breakfast to Market Street and from thence to the river at the fish market then back to Market Street to 8th Street where we went in a barber shop and got a couple of niggers to barber our faces, after which we went down to Mr. Biles. From thence we went to the **State House**[155] in company with Father Hill and Mr. Biles where we staid a short time to hear the lawyers. I went after dinner to Nick's Bank and caused the old fellow to smack down his knuckles, after which I went up to see about the horses and then returned to Mr. Biles' where we staid all night. It rained the principal part of the night.

The scenes of this day has offered very little amusement except the market which was extensive, filled with all manner of vegetables that the country could produce. Fruit in abundance, peaches, apples, pears and diverse others too tedious to mention. The market extends from the wharf to 8th and 9th, a distance of near a mile. In short, you cannot go amiss for market in this place for at every public house, in the wagon yard and all along the sidewalk they string out for the purpose of selling.

We went to the keeper of the State House and asked permission to go to the top of the steeple. But he said he could not let anyone go up in consequence of the rain and hard wind eating in at the doors of the steeple that would necessarily have to be opened that we might see out over the town.

Thursday morning 27th. We rose early and consulted which course to pursue and concluded that I would go and get the horses while the others staid and took breakfast at the tavern. Here I found John Hendrickson who went with me to Mr. Biles'. We left this place after taking leave of the family and started for the **Navy Yard**.[156] We stopped at the entrance and asked permission of the guard to go in, which he granted. We tied the horses and left them standing in the street. After passing the guard at the entrance the next was a soldier who appeared to be completely armed with musket and bayonet and dressed in a soldier's uniform. John Hendrickson was a little before the rest of us when the soldier in authentic but civil manners beckoned to him to come there. He then asked where he was going and what his business was and the company that he had with him. After giving him the satisfaction he wanted, we passed through the yard where there was a cannon and cannon balls in abundance from 6 to 36 pounders.

We were met by, as I supposed, the commandant of the yard and asked permission to go into the houses that are for the purpose of building vessels of war in. There are two of those houses, one of which the ship *Pennsylvania* was built in. That house is empty at present. The other is called a frigate house. This has a vessel called a frigate in it, unfinished.[157] The aforesaid officer looking gentleman called to a man and told him to go unlock the door and open the window that we might

The Philadelphia Navy Yard was located in the Southwark area of Philadelphia from 1801 to 1876

Figure 50. The USS *Dale*, a 16-gun frigate, was under construction in the Frigate House when Henry and the family visited the Navy Yard. *Dale* was launched on October 8, 1839, and sailed to Norfolk to be made ready for sea.

61

have the opportunity of seeing. We went in and went up the flight of stairs built for the purpose of getting on board. This vessel is about as high as a 4 story house. We went on board, and after viewing it from bow to stern and from top to bottom and outside and in, went down. This is what is called a 16-gun frigate. The holes that were left for the masts were about 3 feet in diameter. We then went through the large house to the wharf where they keep a small sail boat called a sea gull in which they keep the sailors and a soldier stands guard to keep them aboard. We saw them take one on board while we were there.

From thence we went up the wharf to near the Exchange, from there we went up to Market Street and then out Market Street so far as the **U. S. Mint**.[158] The day being damp and cloudy they would not grant any admittance. They said a fair morning between 9 and 12 o'clock we could have admittance. This is a spacious looking edifice built of marble and enclosed with an iron railing. It is situated on the west side of the center square. Fronts on Chestnut Street and occupies the ground to Market street between 13th and Broad street.

We then went down Chestnut Street to 3rd where I got out of the wagon and went to the Manufacturers & Merchants Bank to see if they could pay gold for one of their notes, but they could not or would not pay one cent in gold.[159] John Hendrickson left us at the Exchange for to take the steamboat for home, or to Trenton. He did not start. After dinner we started to walk out to buy some few articles. We met John H. and he went with us round the Market Street as far as 4th Street. Father and myself purchased each a hat and a whip and the women bought some few little unspeakables and then went back to the tavern. John H. started for home on the cars at half past 5 in the evening. After supper Father and myself went out to Market Street down to the river, took a dose of oysters. Went up Chester Street, called a few minutes at an auction room. The follow told some

Figure 51. The United States Mint was established in 1792 when Philadelphia was still the nation's capital. The building shown here, the second to house the Mint in Philadelphia, was opened in 1833 and located at the corner of Chestnut and Juniper streets.

Under the Specie Circular Act, which was in effect until 1842, banks were not permitted to pay gold for their notes.

very long yarns about the goods. We left that and went to the tavern and went to bed.

Friday morning 28th. Rose at half past 6, all well except Mother. She complains of pain in her stomach. After breakfast we called for our horses, paid our bill for 13 meals, keeping the horses, from Tuesday evening till Friday morning. The whole bill was $6.00. Then started and went out by the state prison, the **Girard College**[160] and back through Kensington to 2nd Street, thence out to a **Mr. Frederic Linck**,[161] where we stopped and took dinner. While we were there, **Mr. Feleton** and his **wife**[162] came it. They are our cousins that we have never seen. They live close by the **Arsenal**,[163] which place I went to visit. From thence we came to Wm. Hendrickson's where we lit about half past 8.

While at the Arsenal I saw them testing metal of some unfinished muskets, the manner in which they done it was first, they put in them a double charge of powder then a wad of paper, a ball, then more paper on top of the ball, then with a copper rammer all is rammed down firm and tight. They are then taken and put in another department in which there is a place of cast iron fluted the size of a musket. This part is laid close to the ground. After they charged a number say from 15 to 25, they then drill powder all along in a little place in which the breach of the musket rests, the last one of which has a lock attached close by the termination of the drill of powder. This is primed, and by means of a wire running through the door the whole is set off together. This house in which they are proved is made of hewed timber about 6 inches thick covered with the same. The balls are shot in a bed of sand fixed by the side of the house for the purpose. This yard is something like the navy yard, a deposit for all kinds of munitions of war.

Saturday morning 29th. All well. Commenced raining sometime in the night and rained till about 3 o'clock. About this time I went with Wm. Hendrickson to

Figure 52. Founder's Hall, Girard College, Philadelphia, Pennsylvania.

Frankford Arsenal, a munitions plant, was established at Tacony and Bridge streets, Philadelphia, in 1816. It was the center of United States military small arms ammunition design and development until its closure in 1977.

A hog scalder was used on a freshly slaughtered pig, to loosen the pig's hair so it could be removed before butchering. An August, 1867, article in *Atlantic Monthly* magazine, commenting on the precision required of the workers in Cincinnati's slaughterhouses, said, "scald a pig ten seconds too long, or in water twenty degrees too hot, and he comes out red as a lobster; let the water be too cool, or keep the animal in it too short a time, and the labor of scraping is trebled."

Trenton and took my watch to a Jeweler, it being somewhat out of order. While he was repairing it, we went to the **State House**[164] where they were holding court. From thence we returned to the shop, got the watch and returned home. Arrived there about 8 o'clock. Father and Mother and Maria went this afternoon to Asher Hill's and I stayed at Hendrickson's.

Sunday morning September 30, 1838. Rose early and started for Asher Hill's. Arrived there about quarter before 7, found them all well. After breakfast we all went to church and heard a discourse from the **Rev. Cooley**.[165] Returned after service to Asher Hill's with Grandmother Hendrickson in company with us. John Hendrickson and wife came in the afternoon. After we had spent some time we started to Elijah Hendrickson's where we staid all night, where we were agreeably entertained till bed time.

Monday morning Oct. 1, 1838. Rose early this morning and found all well in reasonable health. We took a walk before breakfast over to Wm. H's farm and returned by his grain barn where we discovered another new thing under the sun. This is what is called a hog scalder.[166] The following is a description. A box of 2 inch plank, 2 feet 11 inches high in the clear, 2 feet and a half wide and 5 feet long. A copper boiler of 4 feet 11 inches long, 10 inches in diameter. This boiler is inserted through the end of the box about an inch and a half from the bottom of the box. At the extreme end of the boiler is an elbow and another small pipe or boiler attached to the larger one 4 inches in diameter which is to carry the smoke. The fire is put in the end of the large boiler. The heat of which is carried round through the small one which comes out through the end of the box where the fire is. Then there is another elbow attached to the end of the small pipe to carry the smoke out of the way. They told us that after the box was filled with water and once hot, that it can be easily kept hot with corn cobs sufficient to slaughter and scald 20 to 30 hogs in half a day.

After breakfast we went in company with Asher Hill to Trenton. Father, Mother, Maria and Grandmother Hendrickson went in the waggon and Asher Hill and myself walked. We left the women in town to visit diverse places. We went to visit the state prison and the axe factory, saw mills, etc. From thence to the widow **Polly Hendrickon's**[167] [in Ewing Township] where we stopped and stayed the evening. We had the company of Mrs. Hendrickson, **Mathilda, Elizabeth, Charity, Mercy** and **Frances Julia.** They are her daughters living at home and **Benjamin** the youngest, all the son she ever had. Mr. [Randolph] Hart who lives on and carries on the farm, **Mr. Elijah Hendrickson, Reuben H.** and their **wives**.[168] These constitute the number of persons that set down to tea. About 10 o'clock we returned to Wm. Hendrickson's.

Tuesday morning October 2. Clear and pleasant. Mother has sick headache very bad. While the women were washing Father and myself went down to Trenton. Heard the lawyers plead a little while, then returned to the smith shop and got 2 shoes on Dick and one on Charley. One 25 cents and the other 12½ cents. Returned and went to **Daniel Hart's**[169] in the afternoon with Wm. H's wife, where we stayed the evening. John H. and wife, Asher Hill and wife and Wm. H. and wife. About half past 10 we left for Wm. H's, and the others to their respective homes.

Wednesday morning 3rd. All well. Cloudy and looks like rain. I went down to Israel Hendrickson's and Father went to Trenton. About 12 o'clock it rained a very light shower. About 4 o'clock we left for **John Hazard's**[170] where we arrived about sunset. The evening was cool and windy and denotes frost very much. About the same time we arrived, **Charles Smith**[171] and his **wife** came. This is one of Hazard's sons in law.

Thursday morning 4th. All well. Clear and cold but no frost. After breakfast we went in company with Mrs. Hazard to visit a **Mr. Enos Titus**[172] living in **Pennington**. While we were there **Maria Bunn**[173] their daughter came to see us.

Figure 53. A threshing machine, 1881.

The threshing machine was chief among labor saving inventions that revolutionized farming. Before its invention, grain was separated from the stalk and husks by beating the stalks with wooden paddles. The grain had to be separated from the chaff by hand. The first practical reaper, patented in 1837 by Hiram and John Pitts, had a rolling conveyor belt and pins that separated the grain. Threshing machines were driven by sind or horse-power, and later by steam. Later, rakes, shakers and fans prepared the grain for market all in the same machine. Combines like these cut the grain, separated it, and even bagged it.

(continued on next page)

After dinner Father and myself went out to the field with Mr. Titus. While there we heard the noise of a threshing machine[174] and went to see its performance. After which we returned to Titus', hitched our horses and started for **Mr. John Hageman's**.[175] Stopped and let Mrs. H. out at her house and proceeded. We arrived at the above place after dark, where we were very agreeably entertained by Mr. Hageman and **Mrs. Boggs**, his sister in law.

Friday morning 5th. All well. Clear and pleasant. Went with Mr. Hageman to the mills near his residence.[176] Then returned and started for Mr. Boggs' where we took dinner, spent some time in friendly intercourse and about 4 o'clock we started for D. Hill's and met B. Hill on the road. He had been to a meeting of the friends of the Administration. Father, Mother and Maria staid at the meeting house and I went to D. Hill's. About 9 o'clock they all came back and about half past 12 we all went to bed.

Saturday morning 6th. Clear and pleasant. We are all well as usual. After breakfast we all started for meeting where we heard a discourse from **Dominy Reese**.[177] After preaching we returned to David Hill's in company with a number of other persons who called for to be fed. In the evening loaded up a number of waggons and started for night meeting where we heard a discourse from a young man by the name of **Wittson**[178] from **Sandy Ridge**. I was very sleepy this evening and trusted to the preacher's honesty to do the subject justice and I, in the company with others, went to sleep and did not awake until the preacher told us he was going to pray. We then scratched open our eyes and after meeting was dismissed we went back. John Hendrickson, his wife and Grandmother Hendrickson came up this morning and went with us [from Ewing Township to David Hill's residence in Amwell]. We got home about half past 9 and took tea and about 11 o'clock retired to rest. It rained a little shower.

Sunday morning 7th. Clear and cool. All well as usual. Father and myself barbered our faces this morning and prepared for meeting. After breakfast we shot the poles for the meeting house where we were again addressed by Wittson the aforesaid priest. I could not trust the honesty of the man today, so I watched him very attentively and thought he could have been corrected a number of times in his remarks and assertions. After his discourse ended an exhortation was given by **Dominy Pollard**,[179] their stationed preacher. After the appointments were made and other arrangements for the further continuance of the meeting we unanimously adjourned till evening. Here we met with Samuel Hill and his wife and son. They returned with us to D. Hill's and took dinner. There were also a number of strangers to us took dinner also. In the evening John Hendrickson and his retinue embarked for home. There came two preachers in the evening, left their horse and carriages and walked to church. Their names were **Bartolette**[180] and **George**.[181] We again assembled ourselves together at the meeting house to hear what those Doctors of Divinity would have to say to the people. Service was introduced by the reading and singing a hymn of prayer by the aforesaid Wittson. Discourse by Bartolette. Exhortations and singing and prayer followed and they adjourned til tomorrow at 10 precisely.

I did not like to trust to this priest's honesty, but sleep overtook me and I was obliged to let him take his own course until I took a nap which lasted til he had got nearly through. He, toward the end of his discourse, raised such fearful yells that it aroused me from a state of stupidity which I was indulging myself in, in such a manner as to make me think the house was coming down about my ears. After dismission, we went home with **Mr. Wm. Young**[182] and his **wife**, where we arrived about 10 o'clock. After tea we retired to bed at 12 o'clock. Cold and clear and appears very much like frost.

Monday morning 8th. Rose about half past 6. All well. Clear and cool with some frost. After breakfast we spend some time in friendly intercourse and

Threshers and reapers took the drudgery out of farm work, but, predictably, farm workers protested and resented losing their jobs as mechanical innovations led the country toward an agricultural revolution. With revolution comes big change, and the American workforce had to change with the times. As machines did more of the farming, the workers funneled into factory jobs, where they created, among other things, machines that did farm work.

concluded to go and pay **John Young** a short visit. We accordingly went over. Staid only about an hour and a half and then returned to Wm. Young's. According to a previous arrangement we were to meet **Miss Hannah Hill**, daughter of Samuel Hill, to go with us to New York, at D. Hill's at about 12 o'clock. It now being about half past 11 we started from Wm. Young's and came to **Henry Young's**, where we called a half hour. Started half past 12 and went up to D. Hill's where we found the aforesaid lady waiting. The family had principally all gone to meeting of which I can give no account. Shortly after we got back they came home and prepared dinner. The women were making the necessary arrangements for going to New York. At about 4 o'clock we started on for a village called **Harlengen** and by **Neshanick Meeting House**. From thence to **Flagtown** and then to **Bainbridge** in the aforesaid place where we arrived about 6 o'clock. This man is a brother in law to Hannah Hill. This is a tavern house and a number of scoundrels have come in to get a horn and are making some racket in consequence of their upper stories being somewhat addled.

Tuesday morning 9th. All well. This morning we left Harlengen for **New Brunswick** where we arrived at quarter past 12. We stopped at **I. Stout's**[183] and took dinner. At 2 o'clock precisely we took the cars for New York. Passing through **Rahway, Elizabethtown, Newark** and **Jersey City**. There we ferried over to **New York** and got into a carriage and went to **Mr. James Townsend's**[184] on Greenwich street, No. 707, for which we paid the fellow two shillings apiece for the 5 of us making $1.25. Our bill of fare from New Brunswick to New York was 5 shillings apiece. Here I will make a few remarks. The bridge over the Raritan River at New Brunswick is so constructed that the railroad cars pass over the top of the bridge while the waggons pass under this bridge. It is so arranged as to let sloops and other vessels with high masts to pass up the river and canal.

End of first volume

This note appears at the end of the typed copy of Henry's journal that the author received from Aunt Nonie. Was this entered by Henry — an indication of, at least, his intention of continuing to create a record of his journey? Was it entered by the relative who typed the copy of the journal — an indication of the fact, possibly, that that person had or knew that there was more of the journal? The answer to either of these questions is unknown.

Expansions

Remember the Miller When You Eat Your Daily Bread

Mills to grind grain and plane lumber were essential building blocks in Ohio's growth and development as the young state evolved from a vast wilderness on the edge of the American frontier into an agricultural powerhouse.

Fast moving streams and the sluices that received runoff from canals were excellent sites for mills. By 1850, there were over two thousand flour mills in Ohio.[185] Interstate trade was easier than ever before, Ohio's crops were shipped to market on the National Road and canals, and eastern merchants shipped tobacco, cloth, tools, tea, and other items to settlers in the west.[186]

Mills were noisy, exciting, dangerous places to work. The turning of wheels and gears was enough to make the whole building shudder. Dust from the grinding process was highly flammable, and explosions and fires were common. Careless workers could be caught by hand or clothing and ground up in the gears. "Killed in his mill" was a common epitaph in churchyard cemeteries.[187]

Figure 54. The Clifton Mill, built in 1802 in Clifton, Ohio, is a working mill and restaurant.

Millers all over America consulted their copies of *The Young Millwright and Miller's Guide* (1795), written by Oliver Evans, for advice on building and operating their mills. Evans is credited with early developments in mass production, which all

69

Figure 55. Keri at Clifton Mill's water wheel.

Figure 56. This millstone, on display outside the Yardley Grist Mill in Yardley, Pennsylvania, shows a 3/4 pattern of furrows.

but eliminated the backbreaking physical labor associated with milling, and made the process cleaner and more efficient.

Grain was raised to the top floor of the mill by an elevator — an endless belt of buckets, each carrying a scoopful up to a conveyor, where the grain was rolled in a machine to separate it from chaff, dirt, and bugs. Another conveyor moved the grain to chutes running down through the floor, which carried the grain down toward a funnel-shaped hopper above a set of millstones. The grain passed through the hopper, its valve controlling how fast the grain flowed in between the stones.[188]

The water wheel, attached with a gear mechanism to a vertical shaft, rotated the upper of the two millstones, cut in a series of furrows, which allowed air to circulate and carry off the heat generated by friction during the grinding process. The furrows also carried the ground flour out and away from the stones and into another bin.[189]

The next elevator carried the flour up to the hopper-boy. The hopper-boy, invented by Oliver Evans, was named for the apprentice who performed this task. Inside the shallow tub of the hopper-boy, a revolving wooden rake cooled and dried the flour before it was swept into another chute and taken to the bolter, which sifted the flour into different degrees of fineness,[190] after which it was bagged and ready for market.

In his remarkable book, Evans describes the entire milling process in detail: how to select a site and build the mill,

Expansions

Figure 57. The chutes and hopper direct the grain into the millstones as shown in this example at Bear's Mill, Greenville, Ohio.

Figure 58. Bear's Mill in Greenville, Ohio, built around 1849, is a working mill and gift shop open to the public.

dress and set the stones and water wheel, and gauge the fineness of the flour. Using Evans' innovations, manual labor in the milling process was virtually eliminated. The miller had but to start and stop the wheel and keep a sharp eye while the grinding was in progress. Evans' ideas and inventions were met with mixed reaction because, on one hand, they reduced the cost and increased the efficiency of the flour-milling process but, on the other hand, they eliminated the jobs of individuals who had carried the sacks of grain from one station to another in the mill and performed other laborious tasks.

Land Speculation and Credit Expansion Lead to Recession and Nationwide Panic!

Article I, Section 8. The Congress shall have power to lay and collect taxes, duties, imposts, and excises, to pay the debts and provide for the common defense and general welfare of the United States. . . To coin money, regulate the value thereof, and of foreign coin, and fix the standard of weights and measures.

Figure 59. Coins of the period.

The framers of the Constitution established a specie monetary system based on coined money to control inflation and avoid the financial problems experienced by the colonies during the Revolution, when the government had met its need for revenue by issuing irredeemable paper money. Under the specie system, bank notes and government-issued paper money could be redeemed for gold or silver coin at the issuing bank or the US Treasury.

President Andrew Jackson despised paper money and opposed the Second Bank of the United States, which controlled the flow of gold and silver and influenced the value of the state-run banks' paper money. Jackson thought the Second Bank corrupt for contributing to the political campaigns of officials who then helped it maintain its power, and he planned to eliminate the Second Bank when its charter expired in 1836.[191]

In 1832, Jackson's political opponent, Senator Henry Clay of Kentucky, teamed with Nicholas Biddle, director of the Second Bank, to re-charter it for an additional 12 years. Jackson vetoed the re-charter bill. Biddle retaliated by raising interest rates, refusing loans, and increasing foreclosures. In response, Jackson moved the US Treasury's gold deposits out of the Second Bank and into state-run banks instead. Jackson denounced the Second Bank of the United States as corrupt and monopolistic, and with too many foreign interests. Jackson's opposition to the Second Bank was a central issue in the 1832 Presidential election, as Jackson's opponent, Henry

Expansions

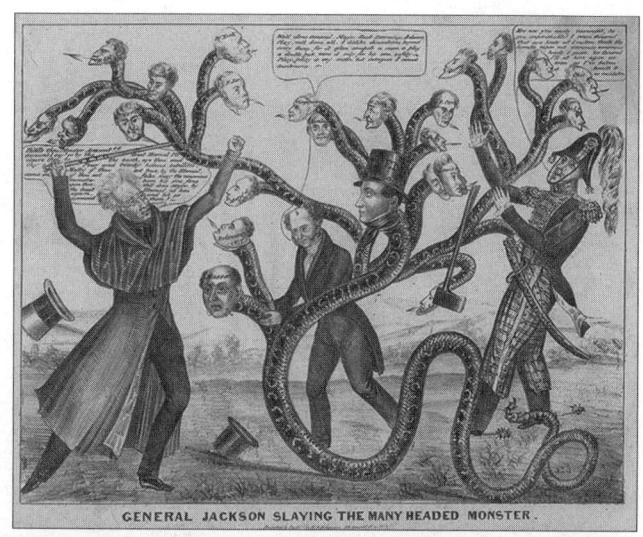

Figure 60. This 1836 political cartoon depicts Jackson slaying the Many-Headed Monster, the Second Bank of the United States.

Clay, was a strong supporter of the Second Bank. Jackson won re-election and took office for another four years.[192]

To further cripple the Bank, Jackson issued the Specie Circular Act of 1836 by executive order. The Act required gold or silver as payment for the purchase of government lands. This Act was intended to curb inflation and protect settlers using devalued paper money to purchase farmland, and has been held responsible for the end of the land boom, the recession, and the Panic of 1837.[193]

In response to the Specie Circular Act, the Second Bank called back specie deposited in state-run banks, and this left the state banks with insufficient gold and silver to back their notes. The state banks called in loans made to settlers and farmers, who, unable to pay their debts, lost their homes and property. The Second Bank of the United States lost its charter in 1836, and, later that year, Biddle secured a charter from the Pennsylvania legislature to operate as a state bank. Though this United States Bank of Pennsylvania remained influential for a few years, it lost money and went bankrupt in 1841.[194]

As always, more than one factor contributed to the country's economic downturn and the Panic of 1837, and some economists and historians absolve Jackson and the Specie Circular Act of any blame. The United States experienced an influx of silver coin from Mexico in the mid-1830s, which was circulated as legal tender and increased the overall specie supply, which in turn led to increased credit, rising prices, and a business boom. The total money supply in the United States rose by 84% from 1833 to 1837, and could have set up conditions for a boom-and-bust cycle.[195]

Specie payments were suspended nationwide in 1837. Limited specie payments resumed in the summer of 1838, which led to a large outflow of coin, and payments were again suspended from 1839 to 1842.

"Elect Martin Van Buren and the National Road is Lost!"

The Whigs and Democrats were locked in hot debate leading to the election of 1840.

The Whig Party, organized in 1833–1834, comprised traditional political enemies who united in their opposition to President Andrew Jackson and his policies. Northern abolitionists despised Jackson because he was a slave owner and advocated the expansion of slavery into new United States territories. Businessmen objected to Jackson's lack of support for banks, specifically the Second Bank of the United States. Farmers and industrialists opposed Jackson's failure to support internal improvement projects, such as turnpikes and canals. The Whigs were held together by a common belief that Jackson would amass power in his own hands, upset the balance between the branches of government, and crush individual liberty. The name Whig conjured memories of the colonists who had opposed British rule and supported the American Revolution. This new political party gave all those in opposition to Jackson's policies a place to gather and oppose what they perceived as tyranny. Kentucky senator Henry Clay, one of the leaders of the Whig movement, was a great advocate of the National Road.[196]

The Whig Party claimed it preferred "liberty to tyranny;" nevertheless, its members believed in a strong federal government that would provide its citizenry with a transportation

Figure 61. A Martin Van Buren campaign poster from the 1840 Presidential Election.

infrastructure to assist economic development. A National Road ticket for the Whig presidential campaign in 1840 warned, "Elect [Democrat] Martin Van Buren and the National Road is lost."[197]

Many Whigs called for government support of domestic business through tariffs that increased the price of foreign goods, thereby making American products more attractive to the consumer. Whigs also believed government should be responsible for the morals of its citizenry by supporting temperance, public education, observance of the Sabbath, and, according to some Whigs, abolitionism.

The opposing Democratic Party believed individual states should retain as much power as possible, and federal powers should consist only of ones absolutely necessary for the federal government to function. Democrats emphasized the rights of the common white people, a message that was especially well received among small farmers and factory workers. The Democratic Party also wanted to open up new land for settlement, a message that struggling farmers and factory workers, who hoped to own their own land someday, welcomed. Though the platform issues haven't changed much, neither Whigs nor Democrats could imagine big government in Washington like we experience today!

Lively political debate must have sprung up at tavern tables all over the country as the election of 1840 approached. Notice how Henry refers to several innkeepers as "Jacksonians" rather than "Democrats."

Figure 62. This 1832 political cartoon shows Van Buren riding on Jackson's back toward the Presidency. Image in public domain.

> **"All hail the Wonderful State of Ohio. Her admission to the Union made possible the construction of the [National] Road."**
>
> — Judge J. M. Lowe (1844–1926)

An overland trade route connecting the waterways of the east with the Northwest Territory had been a dream and a goal of statesmen and citizens since the 1750s. New settlers needed a reliable way to get to the west, and a way to ship produce to eastern markets.

George Washington worried that without an overland trade route, settlers in the west would feel disconnected from the new nation and form commercial and political ties with the Spanish settlements in Louisiana Territory or the French settlements in Canada. In 1784, Washington wrote that the nation should "open wide a door and make a smooth way for the Produce of that Country to pass to our Markets before the trade may get into another channel."[198]

Thomas Jefferson also recognized the need for a road connecting the east and west, but insisted that federal financing of internal improvements was unconstitutional. Many lawmakers from Georgia and the Carolinas agreed — and argued against financing a road that would not benefit the entire country. In fact, the most hotly debated issue in the early 19th Century was whether the federal government had the right to appropriate money for internal improvements.[199]

Albert Gallatin, Secretary of the Treasury under President Jefferson, suggested that the states exempt government land sold in Ohio from taxation for ten years, then use five percent of the net proceeds of the land sales for the construction of roads, "first from the navigable waters emptying into the Atlantic to the Ohio, and afterwards continued through the new State." The 1802 Act enabling Ohio's admission to the Union contained provisions for the construction of such a road from east to west.[200]

Four years later, legislation was passed that launched the National Road project. Construction of the easternmost portion of the road, from Cumberland, Maryland, to Wheeling, Virginia, began in 1811, after many arguments to determine the most favorable route. This portion of the road was specified to be 66 feet wide, with grades not to exceed 5 degrees, and the center 20 feet to be covered with stone, earth, gravel, and sand, or some combination thereof.[201]

During the War of 1812, the British blockade crippled US ports and supply routes, and the primitive nature of the country's inland transportation routes became obvious. Following the War of 1812, the nation began a vigorous road and canal construction campaign which included efforts to complete the National Road.[202]

After the eastern portion of the National Road was completed as far as Wheeling, Virginia, in 1818, the project ground to a halt. Proponents of the road argued that federal funds had been allocated for piers, lighthouses, and beacons to aid travel and commerce when all the states bordered on the Atlantic. These proponents argued that new states in what had been the Northwest Territory should rightfully be granted government funds for road projects.

President James Monroe suggested that internal improvements fell under the "general welfare" clause and were therefore constitutional, as the whole nation would benefit from the construction. In 1824, Monroe signed a bill into law that provided funds to repair the road between Cumberland and Wheeling, and extend it into Ohio. On March 3, 1825, Congress gave $150,000 to build the first section of the National Road in Ohio, from the Ohio River at Wheeling to Zanesville. The groundbreaking ceremony took place on July 4, 1825, at Saint Clairsville.[203]

In 1829, President Andrew Jackson promised the construction of highways, and though the new construction was carried out as planned, the federal government began turning the roads over to the states to maintain. The completed portion of the National Road was heavily traveled and some sections were badly in need of repair. As the states accepted their portions of the road, they began to collect tolls for maintenance and repairs. Portions of the road in Ohio were turned over to the state as early as 1831.[204] The National Road reached Columbus in 1833.

Construction continued westward during the ensuing years through Indiana and Illinois. Congress made its last appropriation to the National Road in 1838, however, and construction of the road stopped in Vandalia, Illinois, in 1839. By this time, the government had spent $6,824,919.33 to build and repair the road.[205]

Figure 63. This bridge, built in 1828, is still open to traffic on a section of the Old National Road west of Zanesville, Ohio.

The National Road, part of a burgeoning network of roads and canals that reached across Ohio, was vital to the state's growth early in the 1830s. According to *ThisWeek* columnist Ed Lentz's article of September 30, 2004, the canals were an "answer to a prayer:"

> The canal was, first and foremost, a mode of transportation. It moved people and goods more easily and cheaply than had previously been the case. The canals started the process that would make Ohio the center of an industrial revolution in the next few years like nothing the world had previously seen... But they were more than that. They also promised a new life and a better future to the people of the state. In that sense, there was something magic about the canals as well.

The groundbreaking for Ohio's canal system occurred, also on July 4, 1825, at Licking Summit. The canal project, like the National Road, began with debate and disagreement over the proposed route. Eventually, two canals were planned to run from Lake Erie to the Ohio River. The Ohio and Erie Canal connected Cleveland with Portsmouth; the first section of this canal opened exactly two years after construction had begun and its entire 308-mile length was completely open to traffic by 1832.[206] The 250-mile-long Miami and Erie Canal was built to connect Toledo and Cincinnati; the section between Cincinnati and Dayton was open by 1830[207] and the last section was completed in 1845.[208]

Epidemics of malaria, inclement weather, and budget problems hampered work on the canals, and in the end, the project cost a whopping sixteen million dollars. To make matters worse, the canals were inoperable during the winter when the water was frozen. Despite their limitations, canals provided passage to and from Ohio's cities and towns, and stimulated interstate trade, especially with merchants in New York. Wheat, which had sold for twenty-five cents a bushel in barter before the canals were in operation, could be sold in New York for five times that price.[209] This was likely a boon to Jediah Hill and Henry Rogers. Perhaps they sought to expand their business in response to the increase in trade and the influx of settlers along the new transportation routes. Businesses from major eastern cities sought Ohio produce, meats, and cheese, and shipped in cloth, coffee, tea, and manufactured goods.

In *Sketches and Statistics of Cincinnati in 1851*, Charles Cist extolled the state's canal system, and declared that although the canal shared business with the Little Miami Railroad in Cincinnati, the railroad was "not expected to reduce materially, or even relatively, the canal business of Cincinnati and vicinity." Though Mr. Cist was optimistic in his predictions for Ohio's canals, "canal fever" peaked less than a decade after the state's two main canals were completed. Revenue receipts for Ohio's canals were at their highest in 1855,[210] after which time the canals' popularity began to wane in the face of more efficient railroads.

Figure 64. A scene along the Ohio and Erie Canal.

Inside the Walls: The Ohio Penitentiary

The concept of rehabilitating, rather than simply punishing, prison inmates had come into vogue early in the 19th Century. The Philadelphia Society for Alleviating the Miseries of Public Prisons, founded by Quakers after the Revolutionary War, originated the concept of penitentiaries where inmates could reflect on their crimes, repent, and thus leave prison rehabilitated.

After the War of 1812, reformers in Boston and New York sought to remove children from jails and have them placed into juvenile detention centers, instead of having men, women, and children imprisoned together.[211]

Auburn Prison in New York, built in 1816, was a penitentiary with single-occupancy cells, where inmates were kept in silent, solitary confinement for their entire sentences. The punishment was harsh, and by 1821, a number of inmates at Auburn had had mental breakdowns or committed suicide.

Within a few years, the prison added labor programs to offset operating costs, which also improved the inmates' morale, as they were allowed out of their cells to work side by side with other inmates during the day. This became the dominant method of prison operation in the United States until about 1870.

Auburn Prison conducted tours for the curious, and the income from admission fees paid the salary of the deputy keeper, a clerk, a turnkey, the chaplain, and a surgeon.[212]

The first state prison in Ohio was built in 1813. In 1815, the Ohio legislature passed the state's first statute punishing larceny by imprisonment. Individuals convicted of larceny of the value of ten dollars or upward could be punished by imprisonment at hard labor for not less than one, and not more than seven, years. Prior to that time, certain crimes, such as larceny, were punishable by whipping. In 1821, the amount before one could be imprisoned for larceny was increased to fifty dollars, but in 1835 that amount was reduced to thirty-five dollars.[213]

The Ohio Penitentiary building that Henry described in his journal was built in Columbus with convict labor between 1832 and 1837, and those prisoners whose sentences would not end before work was completed were promised pardons if they performed the tasks assigned to them and made no attempt to escape. When completed, 1,113,462 days of convict labor had gone into the building of the Ohio Penitentiary, and none of the convict workers violated their agreement.[214]

The Ohio Penitentiary operated under the Auburn System. Prisoners wore striped suits and had their hair cut short. Discipline was exceedingly strict. Prisoners marched from their shops to the dining room and back to their shops in lockstep, and were not permitted to speak to each other except in the presence of their keepers, and then in relation to their work only.[215] Illiterate prisoners were required to attend night classes and all inmates took part in religious services each Sunday. Humane treatment was considered beneficial, as "measured by the cooperation and morale of the prisoners."[216]

Some contemporary reports extolled the benefits of the Auburn Prison System and its application at the Ohio Penitentiary:

> *Piece work [is] given out to the convicts, who are thus stimulated to greater industry, and many of them, by increased application to their labors, often leave the prison upon the expiration of their sentences with sufficient money saved...to start them in useful callings. During our visit mention was made of one prisoner who will shortly leave with $540 earned in that way. The habits of industry thus acquired ... cannot fail to have a beneficial effect upon criminals and do much toward making them honest and industrious citizens... Prisoners who are experienced in any particular trade upon entering the prison are given work in their specialty; but the majority of the convicts have never learned trades when first imprisoned.*[217]

The Ohio Penitentiary was demolished in 1998, and the site is now home to Nationwide Arena. The Arena occupies the former parking lot of the Penitentiary, and the Arena's parking lot occupies the former site of the prison.

Stage Coach and Tavern Days in Mount Sterling

Judith Lowther, owner of Smith House Antiques in Mount Sterling, Ohio, provided this recollection by Amelia Smith Ackerman, dated 1945.

In the year 1808, Great Grandfather Edward Smith came from eastern Pennsylvania with his bride Martha Watson,

Figure 65. 1900 Census records for Falls Township in Muskingum County, Ohio, list Alexander Smith, his wife Malinda, and their four daughters: Ethel, Lillian, Amelia, and Gladys. All are shown here, along with Grandmother Amelia Smith.

and settled in their log house just east of the present Smith homestead, which lies just five miles from the county courthouse in the city of Zanesville, Ohio.

When the news went out that the government was building a highway through to St. Louis, Mo. and opening up a right-of-way through his land, he laid plans for a more pretentious dwelling, one of sandstone blocks. It was built with three stories, patterned after those he had admired in eastern PA. Labor was cheap and a rather pretentious home was made for his family for the period and our local which was in the year of 1830.

Grandfather had his public room downstairs and I can imagine many a tale was told there in front of the huge fireplace with the great logs piled high; the men with their pipes and the barrels piled nearby. I have a license taken out in 1842 by Edward Smith permitting him to sell liquor the cost of which was $10.00.

In the '30s and '40s almost every house along the road was a tavern to accommodate the many wagon teams that were moving over the new pike. Wagon teams with four to six horse hitch were not an uncommon sight, as this was the only means of transportation west except the river routes. A few rods from great grandfather's and due west was another stone tavern owned by Squire Uzal Headley. Between the two houses was a huge barn or shed, which housed the drovers' herds of stock and horses.

Figure 66. The Uzal Headly Inn in Mount Sterling, Ohio, was built around 1802, with an addition built in 1830. It is now a private residence.

In the book *Ohio Builds a Nation* by Samuel Harden Stills (1939), there is an entry titled "One of Ohio's Oldest Inns" about the Headley Inn (1802):

About five miles west of Zanesville, on the old National Pike, is the famous Headley Inn. It sits in a picturesque location surrounded by hills that roll off into prairies. Many of the facts about its early existence have been lost. The old section of the Inn was erected in 1802, or thereabouts.

In 1830 a new section was added, according to a capstone above one of its doors. The structure is made of hewn stones and its walls are sixteen inches thick. The first floor was used as a dining room and bar. Its mammoth stone fireplace is still in perfect preservation.

At first the place was known as the Five Mile Inn — as the five mile post on the Pike was located directly across from its door. In early days it was a rendezvous for cattle drovers, sheep herders, pioneers, and now and then a gentleman of higher calling.

In the days when "old man Headley" owned and operated the tavern, trouble was often caused among drovers and neighbors by a pack of fifteen hounds owned by his two sons, Melim and Helim, of which songs and legends survive to the present.

The old Inn has been resurrected after resting undisturbed for over half a century. Dust has been brushed from its beams, cobwebs removed from its ceilings, floors scrubbed and fires re-lighted. Out in front among shrubs and flowers, an old sign: "Headley Inn" squeaks musically in the wind. Two enterprising daughters of Alexander Smith have opened its doors again to the public.

~

"Take some tree sap and chili peppers and call me in the morning."

The folk remedies described in Henry's journal sound distasteful, ineffective, and downright dangerous — yet these concoctions use ingredients recognized for their healing properties today.

"Number 6," also known as Rheumatic Drops or Hot Drops, a popular medicine in the 19th Century, was a tincture of capsicum and myrrh created by mixing herbs with ethanol. Tinctures provided the strongest possible concentration of the herbs' healing qualities, and retained their potency years longer than drugs in powder form.[218]

Capsicum, or cayenne pepper, has been used for centuries to increase blood flow and is known to increase metabolism and strengthen the immune system. Cayenne pepper is used today in colonic cleanses.

According to *King's American Dispensatory*, published in 1898, capsicum was a "perfect cure" for delirium tremens, as it enabled the stomach to take and retain food, and prevented vomiting.[219] It also steadied the patient, got the blood moving, and promoted sleep. The *Dispensatory* recommended that liberal doses of "Number 6" be administered orally, in tea, or as an enema whenever the patient desired a drink of alcohol.

Myrrh, the dried sap of the tree *Commiphora myrrha*, is most commonly used in traditional Eastern medicine for rheumatic, arthritic, and circulatory problems. In modern Western medicine, myrrh is used in mouthwashes and toothpastes for prevention and treatment of gum disease. It is also used in salves applied to minor abrasions.[220]

In *Vitalogy, or Encyclopedia of Health & Home Adapted for Home and Family Use*, indigo is recommended for treating scarlet fever, typhus, and typhoid fever. Indigo can be mixed with lard and applied externally to wounds, or taken internally.[221] The Archive of American Folk Medicine lists a mixture of indigo, honey, and castor oil as a remedy for worms.[222]

The stagecoach driver who looked at Charley, one of Henry's horses, thought he had a "touch of bots" which is a parasitic infestation of a host by the larvae of the botfly. *Vitalogy* listed several remedies for treating bots, including milk and molasses, castor oil, linseed oil, and alum.[223]

"Virtue, Liberty and Independence"

These words are inscribed on the southwest side of the monument in the Revolutionary Soldiers Cemetery on Ridge Road in East Vincent Township, Chester County, Pennsylvania. The northeast side of the monument reads:[224]

Sacred to the memory of Twenty-two Revolutionary Soldiers, who in the fall of 1777, when the American Army had encamped at the Valley Forge, were lodged in the German Reformed Church (in sight) then occupied as an hospital; who there, distant from their homes, uncomforted by friends and kind relations, deceased in the spring of 1778, of a fever then prevailing in the camp; who were interred in this ground and where they slumbered in their peaceful but neglected tomb (except that Mr. Henry Hipple, Sr. preserved the ground) until the Union Battalion of Volunteers of Chester County, aided by the generous and patriotic people of this vicinity, resolved to have them enclosed and a monument placed over them; the foundation of which accordingly was laid on the 19th of November, 1831, upon which occasion regular military ceremonies were observed, and a funeral oration delivered, to perpetuate the profound regard due in individuals who paid the forfeit of their precious lives for our sacred rights, and for privileges which they were never permitted to enjoy, and to contribute to generations unborn, the memory of the precious price of the Liberty & Independence of our happy Union. They have raised this monument on the 25th of October, 1833, and which

Figure 67. The Revolutionary Soldiers Cemetery, East Vincent Township, Pennsylvania.

Figure 68. Twenty-two soldiers of the Revolutionary War are buried in this cemetery.

Figure 69. This plaque identifies the Revolutionary Soldiers Cemetery as a registered historical landmark.

they also dedicate to the memory of a number of other Revolutionary Soldiers who, the same time and same manner, deceased in the Lutheran Church (then used as a hospital and are buried near it and in other places in this vicinity).

The Revolutionary Soldiers Cemetery on Ridge Road in East Vincent Township is maintained by the township's Historical Commission. A stone wall had been built around the cemetery in 1831. During the 1990s, resident Carl McIlroy became a driving force behind an eight-year project to rebuild the old stone wall, which was completed and rededicated on July 4, 1997. McIlroy built the flagpole that now stands next to the monument inside the cemetery. He also spearheaded efforts to get ownership of the land for the township so that it can be preserved for future generations.

High Fashion and Homespun: Dress in the 1830s

Across the country, women kept up with the fashions of the day by reading magazines like *Godey's Lady's Book*, which made its debut in 1830. Godey's, the best-known women's publication of the day, was edited by a woman, Sarah Josepha Hale, from 1837 to 1877. The magazine included poetry, articles, sheet music, instructions for a garment that could be sewn at home, and a hand-tinted fashion plate in each issue. Early in the 1830s, gigot, or leg-o-mutton, sleeves were popular, and skirts were full, bell shaped, with waistlines just above the natural waist. The favored female silhouette looked like two triangles, with the breadth in the shoulders and hem accentuating the narrow, corseted waist.[225]

Later in the 1830s, fullness in the upper sleeve went out of fashion and the sloping shoulder became preferred. Sleeves were full at the bottom until the end of the decade. Embroidered pelisses (lightweight capes) and pleated bodices were favored. Wide-brimmed bonnets trimmed with silk flowers and feathers framed the face. The fullness of the skirts increased through the 1830s as the approaching era of the hoopskirt lurked on the horizon.

Though there was a great variety of fabrics available in settled areas and on trade routes, people living in more remote locales needed to raise the raw materials necessary to clothe themselves. Wool and linen were the most common fabrics on the frontier. When creating garments from scratch, a family's clothing needs had to be anticipated a year in advance.

A quarter acre of flax could produce enough linen to clothe a large family.[226] The tough stalks were cut and soaked in a pond or trough until they could be broken open and the fibers inside removed. The fibers were combed over boards studded with tacks or metal teeth, to work out the tangles and ready the fibers for spinning.[227]

Spinning filled every spare minute of the fall and winter. Women and girls twisted the loose fibers between their fingers as they pumped the treadle on the spinning wheel with their foot. The wheel turned and drew the twisted thread onto

Figure 70. Morning dress of striped silk at left, white satin evening gown at right — both fashion plates of 1838.

a whirling spindle. The finished thread was dyed, using berries, roots, or nut hulls. The dye was "fixed" to keep it from fading, by boiling it with tannic acid, alum, sodium chloride, or even urine. Chalk, clay, and crushed bone were other substances that could also be used as inert binders.[228]

The finished thread might be sent to a weaver, if there was one in the area. If the lady of the house was doing her own weaving, the thread was strung on her loom.

Carding, or dragging bits of wool back and forth on paddles with small metal teeth to remove the tangles, prepared the wool for spinning. The finished woolen cloth was scoured in urine, or "wash," which was a source of ammonium salts. Fuller's Earth, a clay-like substance, was used with the wash. Fulled woolen cloth treated with lanolin is water resistant, air permeable, slightly antibacterial, and resists odor.

The fulled cloth was then treated with heat, water, and agitation to shrink the fibers. In order for the fibers to shrink evenly, the fabric was beaten with clubs or hammers, or even with feet, at a "wool waulking." Lastly, the cloth was stretched on a wooden frame to shape it before it was cut and sewn into clothing.[229]

The family seamstress could use existing garments as patterns or guides to create patterns, then set out to stitch the family's clothing by hand. Though sewing machines were in existence in 1832, they were not at all common until Elias Howe's machine came out in 1846.

The first commercially prepared sewing patterns were hand drawn. Cardboard templates for children's frocks were available in the early 1860s. Ebeneezer Butterick marketed garment patterns for men and boys beginning in 1863, and for women in 1866.

Delinator first sold blank tissue-paper with instruction booklets for various garments in 1873, but stamped patterns as we know today did not appear on the market until 1919.[230]

"It is a hard life aboard a Man-O-War"
— Captain C. Garrett, USS *Dale*,
at sea, near the equator, 9th January, 1841.

Philadelphia's port and its rivers, located strategically between the southern colonies and New England, had been focal points in the struggle for American independence, and the city had been a leading shipbuilding center for years before the Philadelphia Navy Yard was established in the Southwark area of Philadelphia in 1801. During the War of 1812, when the British burned the Washington Navy Yard and moved against Baltimore, Philadelphia took on a prominent role in the defense of the Atlantic.[231]

Philadelphia's Navy Yard produced, among others, the 120-gun ship-of-the-line *Pennsylvania*, America's largest wooden and sail warship. The construction of *Pennsylvania* dominated the Navy Yard for 15 years and employed over 100 carpenters and 170 mechanics. *Pennsylvania* was launched on July 18, 1837, and made but one voyage, that to Norfolk, Virginia. There it was laid up until 1861 when it was burned to prevent capture by the Confederates.[232]

The Navy Commissioners, augmenting their fleet for services abroad during the 1830s, called for a smaller class of sloops-of-war. Naval engineer John Lenthall's designs were chosen for what eventually became known as the *Dale* class of frigate. The *Dale* class ships were among the last sailing vessels of war constructed in the United States. *Dale* and the four other ships of the class, *Decatur*, *Preble*, *Marion*, and *Yorktown*, were all constructed at different Navy Yards, and all launched in 1839.[233]

Dale was based in Valparaiso, Chile, to protect American commerce and the whaling trade. She returned to the east coast in 1843 and was refitted for a second cruise to the Pacific. In 1846, *Dale* returned to Valparaiso and patrolled the coast until ordered north for duty in the Mexican War. *Dale's* arrival at the bay of La Paz was instrumental in Colonel Burton's defeat of the Mexicans at Todos Santos. During the remainder of the war, *Dale* captured several Mexican privateers and merchant vessels.

Figure 71. USS *Pennsylvania*, America's largest wooden warship, was a 120-gun ship-of-the-line, built at the Philadelphia Navy Yard, and launched on July 18, 1837.

The following is an excerpt from a letter written by the *Dale*'s commanding officer to his wife, during the ship's maiden voyage:

DALE, AT SEA, NEAR THE EQUATOR, 9ᵀᴴ JAN. 1841...
It is a man's motive and actions that drive him away from the comforts of home for a distant quarter of the globe and with the privations of a life at sea... I want to do what others have done in my rank and secure a future promotion, which will be for me and my family. Now at sea, I am suffering severely from illness hoping that our stay at Rio will help regain my strength... It is a hard life aboard a Man-O-War. You must take care of the house and the boys. The Dale *is a fine ship and much faster than the* Yorktown.
— *Capt. C. Garrett*[234]

In August, 1849, *Dale* returned to ordinary in New York for a year, then made three voyages to the African coast to suppress the slave trade, until going out of commission in 1859. She was re-commissioned in June, 1861, and joined the South Atlantic Blockading Squadron, capturing two schooners on the way to Port Royal, SC. During the Civil War, *Dale* served as a store ship in Key West. After the war, she was reassigned as a training ship at the Naval Academy until 1884, then as a receiving ship at the Washington Navy Yard. *Dale* was transferred to the Maryland Naval Militia in 1895, renamed *Oriole* in 1904, and transferred to the Coast Guard at Baltimore in 1906.[235]

Figure 72. The USS *Dale* at harbor in La Paz, Mexico, along with Mexican ships. Painted by William H. Meyers, a gunner on *Dale*. The original of this painting is in the Franklin D. Roosevelt Library, Hyde Park, New York.

Endnotes for Prologue and Section I

1. Arthur J. Peterson, Chairman, Mount Healthy Sesquicentennial Celebration Committee. *Once Upon a Hilltop: Mount Healthy Area Sesqui-Centennial 1817–1967*, p. 12. The first school building or structure in the area was a log cabin, which stood on the site of what is now a private residence at 1500 Compton Road in Mount Healthy. The date of the first term of school is unknown, but the structure was among the first erected after the village of Mount Pleasant was settled in 1793. The village school had student desks facing all four walls and the teacher's platform in the center of the room. Students faced the teacher to recite and the wall to study.

2. United States Federal Census Year: *1860*; Census Place: *Waynesville, Warren, Ohio*; Roll: *M653_1047*; Page: *86*; Image: *175;* Family History Library Film: *805047*. Scott C. Beal, *Anderson Family History*, Family Tree Maker, (2004), pp. 3, 7, accessed September 25, 2011; *http://familytreemaker.genealogy.com/users/b/e/a/Scott-C-Beal/PDFGENE5.pdf*. William H. Anderson, born about 1791, was a physician in Warren County, Ohio, and Eliza Hill's first cousin. His father, David Anderson, was a brother of Rachel Anderson Hendrickson, Eliza's mother.

3. *The History of Miami County, Ohio* (Chicago: W. H. Beers & Co., 1880), Biography 1022; Beal, *Anderson Family History*, p. 4. J. Duer was Joshua Anderson Duer, Eliza Hill's first cousin on her mother's side. Joshua's mother, Charlotte Anderson, was a sister of Rachel Anderson Hendrickson, Eliza Hendrickson Hill's mother. Joshua Anderson Duer was a blacksmith, and owned farmland located in Miami County, Brown Township, in the NW quarter of Section 13.

4. United States Federal Census Year: *1850*; Census Place: *Staunton, Miami, Ohio*; Roll: *M432_711*; Page: *27A*; Image: *296*; William Arrott, C. E., *Map of Miami County, Ohio from Actual Surveys*. (Cincinnati, OH: S. H. Matthews, Publisher; Middleton, Strobridge & Co., Lithographers, 1858). William Hart, born in New Jersey, came to Ohio with his family. His farm was located in Miami County, Staunton Township, in the SW quarter of Section 8.

5. *The History of Miami County, Ohio,* (Chicago: W. H. Beers & Co., 1880), Biography 1070. Oliver Wharton married Jane Duer, another of Eliza Hill's first cousins. Wharton was a wheelwright. His farm was located in Miami County, Brown Township, in the SW quarter of Section 25, adjacent to the town of Fletcher.

6. Beal, *Anderson Family History*, pp. 1, 4. Aunt Charlotte was Eliza Hill's aunt, mother of Joshua and Jane Duer.

7. Leonard Hill and Louise Hill, "Descendents of Paul Hill and Rachel Stout through Charles Hill," (unpublished manuscript in possession of the author, 1953), p. 4. Enoch Drake married Rachel Hendrickson, Eliza Hill's sister.

8. *The History of Miami County, Ohio,* (Chicago: W. H. Beers & Co., 1880), Biography 1066. George Suber married Elizabeth Duer, Eliza Hill's first cousin. His farm was located in Miami County, Brown Township, in the NW quarter of Section 8.

9. Beal, *Anderson Family History*, pp. 1, 3. James Anderson was Charlotte Duer's brother, and Eliza Hill's uncle.

10. Ibid., pp. 1, 3. David Anderson was another of Charlotte Duer's brothers.

11. Ibid., p. 3. These four are sons of David Anderson.

12. William C. E. Arrot, *Map of Miami County, OH from Actual Surveys.* (Cincinnati, OH: S. H. Matthews, Publisher; Middleton, Strobridge & Co., Lithographers, 1858); ibid., p. 9. The Worthington family lived next door to George Suber in Brown Township, in the SW corner of Section 9. George Worthington married Esther Anderson, who was a daughter of David Anderson.

13. Wikipedia, "Tyre," last modified June 24, 2011; http://en.wikipedia.org/wiki/*Tyre*. The outer part of a wheel in British English. Chiltern Open Air Museum online, "The Victorian Blacksmith," excerpted from Fred Archer, ed., *The Countryman Cottage Life Book,* (David & Charles, Publishers, 1974), accessed December 17, 2011; http://www.coam.org.uk/images/workshop%20pdf/KS1workshops/Blacksmith.pdf.

14. United States Federal Census Year: *1850*; Census Place: *Wayne, Warren, Ohio*; Roll: *M432_737*; Page: *371B*; Image: *71*; Beal, *Anderson Family History*, p. 3. Aunt Deborah Anderson was James Anderson's wife.

15. Beal, ibid., p. 4. Possibly Ephriam Anderson was a son of James Anderson. Though his name is spelled Ephriam in the typewritten copy of the journal, in the original draft of the journal, it may have been spelled Ephraim, a more common spelling.

16. United States Federal Census Year: *1860*; Census Place: *Johnson, Champaign, Ohio*; Roll: *M653_942*; Page: *241*; Image: *485*; Family History Library Film: *803942*. Asa Scott, another neighbor, was born in New Jersey.

17. Helen Maitland McLellan, "Old Mills and Their Builders," (Paper presented to the Champaign County Historical Society, Urbana, Ohio, March, 1938). This mill was most likely the Miller/Norman/Old Wiant Mill, built around 1815, located on the north side of Route 36 at the junction of Route 36 and Nettle Creek in Mad River Township, Ohio.

18. Ibid. This mill was most likely the Kite/Roherer/Bryan Mill, built around 1835, located an eighth of a mile north of Route 36, on the east side of River Road in Mad River Township, Ohio.

19. Wikipedia, "Shinplaster," last modified July 9, 2011; http://en.wikipedia.org/wiki/Shinplaster.

20. Marc McCutcheon, *The Writer's Guide to Everyday Life in the 1800's.* (Cincinnati, OH: Writer's Digest Books, 1993), p 14. A dogery, or doggery, is a cheap drinking establishment.

21. Champaign County, Ohio, accessed September 26, 2011; http://champaignoh.com/stay-and-play/recreation/49.html. In preglacial times, the valleys of western Ohio were broad and worn down to an advanced state of erosion. The loose, gravelly soil Henry described comprised drift, pushed ahead of the Wisconsinan glacier that covered Ohio between 14,000 and 24,000 years ago. Cedar Bog, which covers 428 acres in Champaign County, is a National Natural Landmark and State Nature Preserve managed by the Ohio Historical Society. Cedar Bog is a fen, a wet, springy site with an internal flow of water, and neutral or alkaline soil. Over fifty plant species and ten animal species that are rare or endangered are found in Cedar Bog. The nature preserve is open to the public. Cedar Bog Nature Preserve, 980 Woodburn Avenue, Urbana, Ohio 43078; 800/860-0147.

22. Wikipedia, "Corduroy Road," last modified September 17, 2011; http://en.wikipedia.org/wiki/Corduroy_road.

23. Robert C. Brown, *The History of Madison County, Ohio.* (Chicago, IL: W. H. Beers & Co., Publishers, 1883), p. 957. Alvah Winchester was a native of New York who, as a child, settled with his family first in Cincinnati, then in Clark County, Ohio. After his father's death, Alvah moved to London, Ohio, where he became the first tailor in that growing community. Winchester married Matilda Barnett on 6 July 1823, purchased Lot 40 in London in 1824, and purchased Lot 24 in Jefferson in 1833. This, the site of his tavern, is located on the SE corner of Main Street and North Center Street in what is now known as West Jefferson. It is occupied by a modern bank building.

24. *Old Northwest Genealogical Quarterly* (Columbus, OH: Published by the Old Northwest Genealogical Society, October 1903), p. 189; Alfred E.

Endnotes for Prologue and Section I

Lee, A. M., *History of the City of Columbus, Capital of Ohio, in Two Volumes* (New York, NY, and Chicago, IL: Munsell & Co., 1892), p. 377. Levi B. Pinney, born 26 November 1805 and died 4 June 1839, was a son of one of the founders of Worthington, Ohio. He married Henry Rogers' youngest sister, Maria. Levi Pinney was a blacksmith who kept a shop on the NW corner of Front Street and Public Alley in Columbus.

25. Glenn Harper and Doug Smith, *A Traveler's Guide to the Historic National Road in Ohio: The Road That Helped Build America* (Columbus, OH: Ohio Historical Society, 2005), p. 4. The National Road, America's first federally funded highway, was authorized by Congress in 1806. Construction began in 1811, and the Road eventually spanned over 700 miles, from Cumberland, Maryland, to Vandalia, Illinois.

26. Online Dictionary, s.v. "Toper," accessed September 26, 2011; www.dictionary.com. Topers are hard drinkers or chronic drunkards.

27. Henry A. Ford, A. M., and Mrs. Kate B. Ford, *History of Hamilton County, Ohio with Illustrations and Biographical Sketches* (Cleveland, OH: L. A. Williams & Co., Publishers, 1881), p. 371. Hannah Burge was Henry's niece, the daughter of his sister, Sarah, who married Michael Burge of Columbus.

28. Henry Howe, LL. D, *Historical Collections of Ohio in Two Volumes* (Cincinnati, OH: The Arthur H. Clark Company, 1904), pp. 645–646.

29. Oxford English Dictionary, s.v. "Girt," accessed October 19, 2011; www.oed.com. Girting is a strap used to encircle part of the body, in this case probably a horse's belly.

30. McCutcheon, *The Writer's Guide,* p. 132. Coopers make and repair wooden barrels and tubs.

31. *Columbus Business Directory, for 1843–4* (J. R. Armstrong and Samuel Medary, Printer, 1843), p. 116. Cadwallader's Farmers and Mechanics Tavern, owned by Thomas Cadwallader, was located at 77 West Broad Street, on the SE corner of Broad and Scioto streets.

32. William T. Martin, *History of Franklin County: A Collection of Reminiscenses of the Early Settlement of the County* (Columbus, OH: Follett, Foster & Co., 1858), p. 383.

33. Ibid., p. 369.

34. *Columbus Business Directory, for 1843–4*, pp. 73–102.

35. Ohio Department of Geological Survey online, "Glacial Map of Ohio: Ohio Department of Natural Resources, Division of Geological Survey," 2005, accessed September 26, 2011; http://www.dnr.state.oh.us/portals/10/pdf/glacial.pdf. Licking County has glacial drift deposits from the Wisconsinan (14,000–24,000 years ago) and Illinoian (130,000–300,000 years ago) glaciers. Henry noticed different qualities of soil as he passed through the drift deposits east of Columbus and continued into the Appalachian Plateau.

36. N. N. Hill, Jr. *History of Licking County, O. Its Past and Present* (Newark, OH: A. A. Graham Publishers, 1881), p. 475; "Preservation 2000" pamphlet compiled by West Licking Historical Society, p. 72. Kirkersville was laid out in 1832 along the National Road in Licking County. Mr. Bazalleel Brown started the first store there, and soon after erected a sawmill. Kirkersville had a gristmill and sawmill at the east end of town along the National Road that were owned first by James Stone, then later by Henry Geiger.

37. Wikipedia, "Turbine," last modified September 20, 2011; http://en.wikipedia.org/wiki/Turbine. Turbines are rotary engines that extract energy from air or water flow and convert it into useful work. A submerged water wheel, which rotates from the force of a stream to turn the gears of a mill, is an example of a reaction turbine.

38. Norris F. Schneider, *Y Bridge City: The Story of Zanesville and Muskingum County, Ohio* (Cleveland, OH: World Publishing Co., 1950), p. 5. The villages of Gratiot, Hopewell, and Mount Sterling developed from traffic on the National Road. Gratiot was named for General Charles Gratiot of the US Engineers, who supervised the construction of the National Road.

39. Harper, *A Traveler's Guide to the Historic National Road in Ohio*, p. 24.

40. Wikipedia, "Jacksonian democracy," last modified September 23, 2011; http://en.wikipedia.org/wiki/Jacksonian_democracy. A Jacksonian supported President Andrew Jackson and his policies.

41. Archer Butler Hulbert, *Historic Highways of America, Volume 10: The Cumberland Road* (Cleveland, OH: The Arthur H. Clark Co., 1904), p. 207. Bids to repair portions of the National Road, and bids to construct tollhouses in Hebron and Jefferson, were accepted at C&T Rogers Hotel on May 1, 1837.

42. Wikipedia, "Y-Bridge (Zanesville, Ohio)," last modified June 26, 2011; *http://en.wikipedia.org/wiki/Y-Bridge_%28Zanesville,_Ohio%29*. Zanesville's Y-Bridge is world famous.

43. Wikipedia, "Coal," last modified September 24, 2011; *http://en.wikipedia.org/wiki/Coal*. Anthracite, known as stone coal, is a hard, compact variety of coal with a high luster. It has the highest carbon content of all coals.

44. Webster's Unabridged Dictionary online, s.v. "Fippenny Bit," accessed September 26, 2011; *http://www.answers.com/topic/fippenny-bit*.

45. Wikipedia, "Appalachian Plateau," last modified August 31, 2011; *http://en.wikipedia.org/wiki/Appalachian_Plateau*. The rolling hills Henry described as he drove through Guernsey County are part of the Appalachian Plateau.

46. Elise Lathrop, *Early American Inns and Taverns* (New York, NY: Arno Press. 1977), p. 347.

47. Online Science Encyclopedia, s.v. "Germ Theory," accessed September 26, 2011; *http://science.jrank.org/pages/3035/Germ~Theory.html*.

48. Thomas B. Searight, *The Old Pike: A History of the National Road* (Uniontown, PA: Published by the author, 1894), p. 300. William Armstrong's tavern was located west of Fairview.

49. Answers.com, McGraw Hill Science and Technology Dictionary, s.v. "Coal Bank," accessed September 26, 2011; *http://www.answers.com/topic/coal-bank*. A coal ba[n]k is a place where a seam of coal is visible in the ground.

50. Dr. Cliff Snyder, Southeast Director of the Potash and Phosphate Institute. *Efficient Fertilizer Use Manual*, (Regional Newsletter, February 2006), p. 2, accessed September 26, 2011; *http://back-to-basics.net/efu/pdfs/pH.pdf*. The acidic soil in the Appalachian region of eastern Ohio has high concentrations of iron, salt, and clay, and is well suited to growing wheat and corn. That region was known for its iron works, salt manufacturing, and pottery production.

51. Wikipedia, "West Virginia," last modified September 26, 2011; *http://en.wikipedia.org/wiki/West_Virginia*. In 1838, what is now West Virginia was part of the state of Virginia. West Virginia separated from Virginia during the Civil War and was admitted to the Union in 1863.

52. Lathrop, *Early American Inns and Taverns*, p. 363; Searight, *The Old Pike*, p. 296.

53. United States Department of Agriculture, Agriculture in the Classroom online, "A Look at West Virginia Agriculture," accessed September 26, 2011; *www.agclassroom.org/kids/stats/westvirginia.pdf*. The soil in the northern neck of West Virginia is shallow, clayey, and acidic. River flood plains provide blacker, more fertile soil, and limestone bedrock helps neutralize acidity.

54. Online Dictionary, s.v. "Donsie," accessed September 26, 2011; *http://dictionary.reference.com/browse/donsie*.

55. Harvey Wickes Felter, M. D., and John Uri Lloyd, Phr. M., Ph.D., *King's American Dispensatory, (1898)*, accessed September 26, 2011; *http://www.henriettesherbal.com/eclectic/kings/index.html*.

56. Searight, *The Old Pike*, p. 284.

57. Wikipedia, "Wheeling Creek," last modified April 5, 2011; *http://en.wikipedia.org/wiki/Wheeling_Creek_%28West_Virginia%29*. Wheeling Creek is a tributary of the Ohio River that originates in western Pennsylvania and flows westward until it joins the Ohio River near Wheeling. As Little Wheeling Creek in Pennsylvania, it winds back and forth across the National Road.

58. Searight, *The Old Pike*, p. 270. Mr. Samuel Hughes' tavern was known for its aristocratic patronage. It is no longer standing.

Endnotes for Prologue and Section I

59. Otto Juettner, A. M., M. D., *Daniel Drake and His Followers Historical and Biographical Sketches* (Cincinnati, OH: Harvey Publishing Co., 1909), p. 29; Boyd Crumrine, ed., *History of Washington County, Pennsylvania, with Biographical Sketches of Many of its Pioneers and Prominent Men* (Philadelphia, PA: L. H. Everts & Co., 1882), p. 476.

60. Wikipedia, "Washington & Jefferson College," last modified September 6, 2011; http://en.wikipedia.org/wiki/Washington_%26_Jefferson_College.

61. Brownsville, Pennsylvania online, "Pittsburgh might amount to something if it weren't so close to Brownsville," accessed September 26, 2011; http://web.me.com/rpday/background/brownsville.html. This covered bridge spanned the Monongahela River.

62. Writers' Program of the Work Projects Administration in the Commonwealth of Pennsylvania, *Pennsylvania: A Guide to the Keystone State* (New York, NY: Oxford University Press, 1940), p. 598.

63. Searight, *The Old Pike*, pp. 247–8. This was the Searight House. William Searight was a Commissioner for Public Works, and left the management of the tavern to others.

64. Cassandra Vivian, *A Driving Tour of the National Road in Pennsylvania*. (Monessen, PA: Trade Routes Enterprises, 1994), p. 21. Originally named Woodstock in 1791, this village was renamed Monroe after a visit from James Monroe in 1816, the year he was elected President. The village is now known as Hopwood.

65. Searight, *The Old Pike*, p. 233. This cut stone building, now part of the Hopwood Fire Department, is located on US Route 40 in Hopwood. It was built in 1818.

66. Wikipedia, "Laurel Hill," last modified August 28, 2011; http://en.wikipedia.org/wiki/Laurel_Hill_%28Pennsylvania%29. Laurel Hill is a 70-mile-long mountain, the westernmost ridge of the Appalachian Ridge and Valley Province in this area. Its average elevation is 2,700 feet, with knobs above 2,900 feet. Its highest point, at Seven Springs Ski Resort, is 2,994 feet.

67. Searight, *The Old Pike*, p. 356. William Downard kept a water trough on Laurel Hill for use *pro bono publico*.

68. Tobacco News and Information online, "Economic Aspects of Tobacco during the Colonial Period 1612–1776," accessed September 26, 2011; http://www.tobacco.org/History/colonialtobacco.html. Tobacco was a staple crop of the Chesapeake region from Colonial times. Maryland farmers grew tobacco to "grow some cash," pay off debt, and rise above subsistence farming. Though the high demand for tobacco helped stabilize the economy, the plants themselves exhausted the soil in as few as three years.

69. Vivian, *A Driving Tour of the National Road*, p. 14. The Petersburg (now Addison) tollhouse is preserved by the Great Crossings Chapter of the National Society of the Daughters of the American Revolution. The seven-sided, cut-stone building was named to the National Register of Historic Places in 1976.

70. Searight, *The Old Pike*, p. 211.

71. Wikipedia, "Keysers Ridge," last modified November 26, 2010; http://en.wikipedia.org/wiki/Keysers_Ridge. The elevation of Keysers Ridge is 2,894 feet.

72. Thompson, *The National Road*, pp. 80–81.

73. Maryland Geological Survey online, "Maryland's Highest Waterfalls and Mountains," accessed September 26, 2011; http://www.mgs.md.gov/esic/fs/fs9.html. The elevation of Meadow Mountain is 3,022 feet.

74. Google Translate, accessed September 26, 2011; http://translate.google.com/#la|en|ad%20captandum. *Ad captandum* translates to "kept to the." Henry may have misused this Latin phrase. The translation of "the match not to be found" is *"Agone, non invenitur."*

75. Wikipedia, "Wills Mountain," last modified September 23, 2011; http://en.wikipedia.org/wiki/Wills_Mountain. The Narrows at Wills Creek, between Wills Mountain, elevation 2,790 feet, and Haystack Mountain, elevation 1,706 feet.

76. Cumberland Road project online, "Scenes from the Old National Road, Allegany County, Maryland," accessed September 26, 2011; *http://www.cumberlandroadproject.com/maryland/allegany/photo-pages/the-narrows-photos1.php*.

77. Hillary Willison, From an untitled, unpublished manuscript on file at the Allegany County, Maryland Historical Society's library. These taverns may have been the Elbin, Stewert, and Street taverns.

78. Ibid. This mill was likely Wolf's Mill.

79. Wikipedia, "Polish Mountain," last modified April 27, 2011; *http://en.wikipedia.org/wiki/Polish_Mountain*. The elevation of Polish Mountain is 1,800 feet.

80. Searight, *The Old Pike*, p. 202. Philip Fletcher's tavern was a log cabin on the north side of the road, and "the table it furnished was equal to the best on the road."

81. Ibid, p. 201. This tavern was probably either the Widow Ashkettle or the Widow Turnbull's tavern.

82. Wikipedia, "Sideling Hill," last modified May 17, 2011; *http://en.wikipedia.org/wiki/Sideling_Hill*. The elevation of Sideling Hill is 2,301 feet.

83. Searight, *The Old Pike*, p. 200. Mr. Brosius' tavern was located at the eastern foot of Sideling Hill. The distance from the foot to the summit of Sideling Hill was four miles, making it the longest hill on the National Road.

84. Ibid., p. 199. The Widow Bevans' tavern was a popular stopping place.

85. Ibid., p. 199. This was probably David Miller's stone tavern in Indian Spring, Maryland.

86. Maryland State Highway Administration online, "Wilson Bridge 1817–19," accessed September 26, 2011; *http://www.sha.state.md.us/Index.aspx?PageId=272*. Henry stated that Wilson Bridge had three arches, but it actually has five. Today, the bridge stands as it did when first completed in 1819.

87. Historical Marker Data Base online, "Wilson's Store: Store of Three Wonders," accessed September 26, 2011; *http://www.hmdb.org/marker.asp?marker=4932*. This is believed to be Huyett Mill, which was located just north of Wilson Bridge.

88. Map of Hagerstown, Washington County, Maryland (J. C. Sidney, Publisher, 1850); Google Maps, Hagerstown, Maryland, accessed September 26, 2011; *www.maps.google.com*. The Rising Sun Hotel was located on South Potomac Street, between Baltimore and West Antietam streets. The site is now occupied by the Washington County Free Library's downtown branch.

89. United States Department of the Interior, National Register of Historic Places Registration Form, Leitersburg Historic District, WA-I-174, dated November 5, 2003, p. 32, accessed October 5, 2011; *http://www.msa.md.gov/megafile/msa/stagsere/se1/se5/020000/020900/020917/pdf/msa_se5_20917.pdf*. John Lahm's tavern was located at what is now 21413 Leiter Street in Leitersburg.

90. "Cross Keys, Near New Oxford, Was Site of Colonial Tavern Century And A Half Ago; Old Buildings Gone," *Gettysburg Times* (Gettysburg, PA), July 14, 1960. The Cross Keys tavern, located at the corner of US Route 30 and Pennsylvania Route 94, was torn down in the 1850s. The tavern sign, dated 1809, was presented to the Adams County Historical Society in Gettysburg in 1960.

91. Katherine D. Quirk, "Black Horse Tavern is former field hospital," *Gettysburg Times* (Gettysburg, PA), April 18, 1983. The tavern Henry mentions was most likely the Black Horse Tavern, located on Marsh Creek, three miles west of Gettysburg. No record has been found to confirm that J. Weigle operated a tavern in Adams County, Pennsylvania. The Black Horse was built in 1812 and was owned by William McClellan until the 1840s. The tavern served as temporary headquarters by Confederate General Robert E. Lee during the Battle of Gettysburg, and was also used as a field hospital for wounded Confederate soldiers.

92. "Index of Tavern License Applications Recommended and Granted For Taverns in What is Now Adams County, Pennsylvania 1749–1899."

Endnotes for Prologue and Section I

Compiled by Diane M. Krumrine, Adams County Historical Society, Gettysburg, Pennsylvania, 2004. James Fink kept a tavern in Adams County, Pennsylvania, from 1838–1840.

93. City of York, Pennsylvania online, "City of York — The First Capital of the United States," accessed September 25, 2011; *http://yorkcity.org/history*. About 1812 Peter Wilt, owner of The Golden Lamb tavern on East Market Street, built a hall. It was the first place of public entertainment in the town of York.

94. No record has been found to confirm that Joshua Taylor operated a tavern in Columbia, Pennsylvania.

95. Jonathon Green, *Cassel's Dictionary of Slang: A Major New Edition of the Market-Leading Dictionary of Slang* (London, England: The Orion Publishing Group Ltd., 2005), p. 1035.

96. Wikipedia, "Wrightsville Bridge," last modified June 4, 2011; *http://en.wikipedia.org/wiki/Columbia%E2%80%93Wrightsville_Bridge*. Railroad cars were drawn across the bridge with horse power to avoid sparks and fire near the wooden bridge.

97. Wikipedia, "Susquehanna and Tidewater Canal," last modified July 1, 2011; *http://en.wikipedia.org/wiki/Susquehanna_and_Tidewater_Canal*. This was the Susquehanna and Tidewater Canal, constructed between 1836 and 1840.

98. Penn State College of Agricultural Sciences, Penn State Extension online, "The Soils of Pennsylvania Part 1: Soil Management," accessed September 26, 2011; *http://extension.psu.edu/agronomy-guide/cm/sec1/sec11a*. The limestone-derived soil of the valleys in the central and eastern Piedmont region of Pennsylvania is some of the most productive in the state. The soil has few rock fragments and good water-holding capability and its erosion potential is low.

99. Lancaster County, Pennsylvania Government online, "A Self-Guided Walking Tour Along Historic King Street from Penn Square to Broad Street," accessed September 26, 2011; *http://www.co.lancaster.pa.us/lancastercity/lib/lancastercity/east_king_walking_tour.pdf*. The Leopard Hotel was located at 105 East King Street between Duke and Queen streets. The building currently located on this site was built in 1912, and functioned as a hotel until the 1980s.

100. "Papers Read Before The Lancaster County Historical Society," Volume 23, No. 1; Friday, January 3, 1919, p. 33. John H. Duchman operated the Leopard Hotel, and changed its name to The Weber in 1839.

101. United States Federal Census Year: *1860*; Census Place: *East Earl, Lancaster, Pennsylvania*; Roll: *M653_1122*; Page: *205*; Image: *210*; Family History Library Film: *805122*. Henry Yunt and his wife, Maria, ran a Tavern in Blue Ball, Lancaster County, Pennsylvania.

102. No record has been found to confirm that David Hasta operated a tavern in Morgantown, Pennsylvania.

103. Online Dictionary, s.v. "Burthen," accessed September 26, 2011; *www.dictionary.com*. Burthen is an archaic term for burden.

104. Lancaster County, Pennsylvania Government online, "A Self-Guided Walking Tour Along Historic King Street from Penn Square to Broad Street," accessed September 26, 2011; *www.cityoflancasterpa.com*. Along East King Street in Lancaster, a walking tour of the block "culminates in a city park that was once the site of a reservoir."

105. Colonial Williamsburg online, "The Fences of Williamsburg," accessed September 26, 2011; *www.history.org/history/teaching/cwfences.cfm*. A pale fence is a picket fence.

106. Penn State University Agronomy Guide online, accessed September 26, 2011; *http://extension.psu.edu/agronomy-guide/cm/sec1/sec11a*. The soil composition in the Conestoga Valley is limestone-derived, and comparable to the soil Henry remarked upon near Columbia, Pennsylvania. The productive soils of the Conestoga Valley are used extensively for agriculture.

107. The Seven Stars Inn online, "History of the Seven Stars," accessed September 23, 2011; *www.sevenstarsinn.com*. The Seven Stars Inn (1736) located on Ridge Road in East Vincent Township, Chester County, Pennsylvania, currently operates as a restaurant.

108. Ibid. The Seven Stars Inn's website lists George Christman as one of the tavern's former owners.

109. The Broad Axe Tavern online, accessed September 24, 2011; http://www.broadaxetavern.com/. The Broad Axe Tavern is located at the corner of Shippack and Butler pikes, and after a complete renovation, reopened as a restaurant in May 2009.

110. Whitpain Township property tax records, on file at the Historical Society of Montgomery County, Pennsylvania. Tax records from 1837–39 show Ann Acuff as innkeeper in Whitpain Township, Montgomery County, Pennsylvania.

111. Reading Railroad online, "RDG Co. — A Breif (sic) History," accessed September 26, 2011; www.readingrailroad.org. The Philadelphia and Reading Railroad Company was established in 1833.

112. J. Smith Futhey and Gilbert Cope, *History of Chester County, Pennsylvania With Genealogical and Biographical Sketches, Volume One.* (Philadelphia, PA: Louis H. Everts. 1881), p. 101. In September 1777, wounded soldiers from the Battle of Brandywine were removed to the German Reformed Church on Ridge Road. A "very malignant fever" broke out among them and many died. Twenty-two soldiers are buried at this site.

113. East Vincent Township, Pennsylvania online, "East Vincent Churches," accessed September 24, 2011; www.eastvincent.org. A different church building now stands at the site of the German Reformed Church. The church used as a hospital in 1777 was a log structure.

114. Northampton Historical Society online, "Endangered White Bear: A History of the Spread Eagle Inn," accessed September 24, 2011; http://www.northamptontownshiphistoricalsociety.org/SpreadEagle/SpreadEagle_history.pdf.

115. Wikipedia, "Yardley-Wilburtha Bridge," last modified January 7, 2011; http://en.wikipedia.org/wiki/Yardley%E2%80%93Wilburtha_Bridge. The Yardleyville-Wilburtha bridge, built in 1835, was a 903-foot-long wooden bridge connecting Yardleyville (now Yardley) Pennsylvania with Greensburg (now Wilburtha) in Mercer County, New Jersey.

116. Hill, "Descendants of Paul Hill and Rachel Stout . . . .," p. 4. John Hendrickson was Eliza Hill's brother. He was born 11 March 1793 and died 30 September 1864. He married Sarah Green 26 December 1818.

117. Hill, "Descendants of Paul Hill and Rachel Stout . . . .," p. 4. William Hendrickson, another of Eliza Hill's brothers, was born 26 November 1800 and died 1880. He married Rebecca Green 26 September 1826.

118. Hill, "Descendants of Paul Hill and Rachel Stout…..," pp. 4, 53. Asher Hill, Jediah Hill's youngest brother, was born 7 January 1798 and died 16 August 1879. He married Rachel Green 19 September 1818, and later, after Rachel's death, married her sister, Margaret Green, on 10 January 1827.

119. United States Federal Census Year: *1860*; Census Place: *Trenton Ward 1, Mercer, New Jersey*; Roll: *M653_698*; Page: *21*; Image: *22*; Family History Library Film: *803698*. This William Hendrickson was John Hendrickson's son, born in 1821. John and William lived in Trenton and had a butcher shop.

120. United States Federal Census Year: *1860*; Census Place: *Springfield, Hamilton, Ohio*; Roll: *M653_979*; Page: *276*; Image: *180*; Family History Library Film: *803979*. Randolph (or Randal) Hunt was one of Eliza Hill's brothers-in-law. He was born about 1799, and married Eliza's youngest sister, Martha. The Hunt family later migrated to Ohio. 1860 Federal Census records show them living next door to the Henry Rogers family in Mount Healthy, Ohio.

121. United States Federal Census Year: *1850*; Census Place: *Ewing, Mercer, New Jersey*; Roll: *M432_454*; Page: *246B*; Image: *509*; Hill, "Descendants of Paul Hill and Rachel Stout . . . .," p. 4. Israel Hendrickson, born 20 March 1803, was Eliza Hill's brother. He married Eleanor Smith. Israel lived in Ewing, Mercer County, New Jersey.

122. This was probably John Hendrickson's son William. No record has been found for Israel Hendrickson having a son named William.

123. Michele S. Byers, Executive Director, New Jersey Conservation Foundation, New Jersey Today online, "Saving Colonial History at Petty's Run,"

Endnotes for Prologue and Section I

accessed September 26, 2011; *http://njtoday.net/2011/09/23/saving-colonial-history-at-petty%E2%80%99s-run/*. Possibly the paper mill currently being excavated in the Pettys Run archeological site between the Old Barracks and the State House in Trenton. Conservatree online "A Brief History of Paper," accessed January 12, 2012; *http://conservatree.org/learn/Essential%20Issues/EIPaperContent.shtml*.

124. Trenton Historical Society, *A History of Trenton 1679–1929: Two Hundred and Fifty Years of a Notable Town with Links in Four Centuries* (Princeton, NJ: Princeton University Press, 1929), accessed September 24, 2011; *http://www.trentonhistory.org/1929history.html*. Possibly some of the many mills built along Assunpink Creek.

125. Ibid. Joseph Moore owned a flour mill in the Mill Hill district of Trenton from 1835–1843.

126. Hill, "Descendents of Paul Hill and Rachel Stout . . . .," p. 3. Benjamin Stout Hill was Jediah Hill's brother, born 23 September 1787 and died 15 April 1844.

127. Ibid., p. 8. Benjamin Stout Hill's son, David, born in 1816, married Ann Sutphen in 1841. Because a later journal entry mentions David Hill, Jediah's brother, this entry seems to refer to the younger David Hill and his fiancée.

128. Hiram Edmund Deats, *Marriage Records of Hunterdon County, New Jersey, 1795–1875* (Flemington, NJ: H. E. Deats, Publisher, 1918), p. 132. Margaret, nee Vandike, married Benjamin Stout Hill in 1809.

129. Hill, "Descendants of Paul Hill and Rachel Stout," p. 8. Jane Hill was born 13 February 1813.

130. Ibid., p. 8. Juliet Ann Hill was born 13 April 1818.

131. Barefoot's World online, "John Hart, Signer of the Declaration of Independence," accessed September 24, 2011; *www.barefootsworld.net/johnhart.html*.

132. Barber, John W., and Henry Howe, *Historical Collections of the State of New Jersey* (New York, NY: Published for the Authors by S. Tuttle, 194 Chatham-Square, 1844), p. 261; Deats, *Marriage Records of Hunterdon County, New Jersey*, p. 132.

133. United States Federal Census Year: *1850*; Census Place: *East and West Amwell, Hunterdon, New Jersey*; Roll: *M432_453*; Page: *24A*; Image: *53*; Hill, "Descendants of Paul Hill and Rachel Stout," p. 52. David Hill, Jediah Hill's brother, was born 28 August 1795 and died 10 February 1865. He was married to Eliza Hill's sister, Mariah. David lived in East Amwell Township, New Jersey.

134. New Market is now known as Linvale.

135. Wikipedia, "Geography of New Jersey," last modified September 24; 2011, *http://en.wikipedia.org/wiki/Geography_of_New_Jersey*. The soil near Trenton, on the Delaware River, is clay loam, loose and unconsolidated, fertile, and suited for orchards, dairy, and general farming. Trenton is positioned on the boundary of the Piedmont and Coastal Plain physiographic regions of the United States.

136. Thomas F. Gordon, *A Gazeteer of the State of New Jersey, 1834* (Trenton, NJ: Published by Daniel Fenton; John C. Clark, Printer [Philadelphia, PA], 1834), pp. 94, 142; Rutgers School of Arts and Sciences, Department of Earth and Planetary Sciences online, "Geology of the Newark Rift Basin," accessed September 26, 2011; *http://geology.rutgers.edu/103web/Newarkbasin/NB_text.html*. The area around New Market, now Linvale, was known, in the 1830s, for its production of corn, grain, and flax. The red rock Henry noticed at New Market, about ten miles north of Trenton, is a red sandstone on a red shale base. Large basins formed in this area from rifting as North America and Africa began to drift apart about 200 million years ago. The basins filled with sediment from surrounding higher ground

137. Rootsweb's World Connect Project online, "Hunterdon Co, NJ, inhabitants 1700–1800," accessed September 25, 2011; *http://wc.rootsweb.ancestry.com/cgi-bin/igm.cgi?op=GET&db=fredericlathrop&id=125879*. Squire Jacob Williamson was born 5 January 1759 in New Jersey. He moved to Amwell Township in 1778 and purchased a mill in Clover Hill and 72 acres. He died 7 July 1841 at 82 years of age.

138. Probably the younger David Hill's mother-in-law.

139. Deats, *Marriage Records of Hunterdon County NJ 1795–1875*, p. 246. Adah Schenck married William Cain on January 6, 1838.

140. The Free Dictionary online, s.v. "Indeterminate," accessed September 26, 2011; http://www.thefreedictionary.com/Indeterminateness.

141. United States Federal Census, Year: 1830: *Amwell, Hunterdon, New Jersey*, Page: *340*; NARA Roll: *M19- 83*; Family History Film: *0337936*. Aaron Prall resided in Amwell Township, Hunterdon County.

142. J. W. Otley and J. Keily, Surveyors, *Map of Mercer County, New Jersey* (Camden, NJ: Lloyd Van Der Veer, Publisher, 1849). If the family were traveling to Aaron Prall's home from David Hill's home, which were both in East Amwell, they would have more likely passed through Wearts Corner.

143. United States Federal Census, Year: 1830: *Amwell, Hunterdon, New Jersey*, Page: *324*; NARA Roll: *M19- 83*; Family History Film: *0337936*. Peter Wilson also resided in Amwell.

144. Joseph Hunt's relationship to the family is unknown.

145. Hill, "Descendants of Paul Hill and Rachel Stout," p. 3. Samuel C. Hill, born in 1787, is Jediah Hill's first cousin, the son of his Uncle James Hill.

146. Eli F. Cooley and William S. Cooley, *Genealogy of Early Settlers in Trenton and Ewing*, p. 120; A History of Trenton 1769–1929 . . . online, "1859 Trenton City Directory," accessed September 25, 2011; http://trentonhistory.org/Directories/1859dir.html. Jane Smith, presumably a sister of Eleanor Smith Hendrickson, and a daughter of Anthony Smith of nearby Lawrence, New Jersey, was listed as a dressmaker with a shop located at 64 Broad Street, Trenton, in the 1859 Trenton City Directory. Henry's journal indicates two Miss Smiths. The full identity of the other sister is unknown.

147. Wikipedia, "Pattern (sewing)" last modified December 10, 2011; http://en.wikipedia.org/wiki/Pattern_%28sewing%29.

148. Beal, *Anderson Family Tree*, p. 2. Rachel Anderson Hendrickson was Eliza Hill's mother.

149. Arrott, *Map of Miami County, Ohio*; Beal, *Anderson Family Tree*, p. 4.

150. Beal, ibid., p. 1; A History of Trenton 1769–1929 . . . online, "1844 Trenton City Directory," accessed September 26, 2011; http://www.trentonhistory.org/Directories/1844DIR.html. Patience Jones and Letitia Clossin Barwis were half sisters, daughters of Mary Anderson, an aunt of Eliza Hill's. John Barwis, Letitia's husband, was listed in the 1844 Trenton City Directory as a tailor with a shop at 7 West Second Street.

151. Beal, ibid., pp. 4–5. Mrs. White was Abigail Anderson White, another aunt of Eliza Hill.

152. Joseph Jackson, *Market Street, Philadelphia: The Most Historic Highway in America, Its Merchants and Its Story* (Philadelphia, PA: The Public Ledger Company, 1914) p. 153. "Right in this block [of Market Street] in a building which still stands at 1008 and 1010, George W. Kendrick . . . kept the White Horse, a farmer's hotel, about fifty years ago."

153. Wikipedia, "Fairmount Water Works" last modified May 30, 2011; http://en.wikipedia.org/wiki/Fairmount_Water_Works. The Fairmount Water Works was the first municipal water system in the United States, designed in 1812 and built between 1819–1822.

154. United States Federal Census Year: *1850*; Census Place: *Trenton East Ward, Mercer, New Jersey*; Roll: *M432_454*; Page: *168A*; Image: *355*. Israel C. Biles, a painter, resided in the East Ward of Trenton in 1850.

155. Independence Hall.

156. Paolo E. Coletta, ed., *United States Navy and Marine Corps Bases, Domestic* (Westport, CT: Greenwood Press, 1985), p. 475.

157. Ibid., p. 477.

158. Wikipedia, "Philadelphia Mint," last modified March 12, 2011; http://en.wikipedia.org/wiki/Philadelphia_Mint

159. Wikipedia, "Panic of 1837," last modified July 11, 2011; http://en.wikipedia.org/wiki/Panic_of_1837.

Endnotes for Prologue and Section I

160. Wikipedia, "Girard College," last modified September 25, 2011; http://en.wikipedia.org/wiki/Girard_College. Girard College, a private boarding school for orphan boys, was established in 1831 and endowed by Stephen Girard (1750–1831). Girard, a French immigrant, was reputedly the richest man in America at the time of his death. His bequest to Girard College was the largest private charitable donation up to that time in American History.

161. Clement Biddle, *The Philadelphia Directory* (Philadelphia, PA: Printed by James & Johnson, 1791), p. 78. Frederick Linck, a stone cutter, resided at 207 Sassafras Street.

162. No records have been found of the Feletons, or Fultons.

163. Wikipedia, "Frankford Arsenal," last modified August 16, 2011; http://en.wikipedia.org/wiki/Frankford_Arsenal.

164. Wikipedia, "New Jersey State House," last modified August 26, 2011; http://en.wikipedia.org/wiki/New_Jersey_State_House.

165. United States Federal Census Year: *1850*; Census Place: *Ewing, Mercer, New Jersey*; Roll: *M432_454*; Page: *238B*; Image: *493*. Reverend Eli F. Cooley was a Presbyterian minister. He coauthored a book entitled *Genealogy of Early Settlers in Trenton and Ewing "Old Hunterdon County" New Jersey*. He died in April 1860 in Ewing, Mercer County, New Jersey.

166. *Atlantic Monthly* online, "Cincinnati," accessed September 25, 2011; http://www.wattpad.com/21871-the-atlantic-monthly-volume-20-no-118-august-1867?p=98.

167. Cooley and Cooley, *Genealogy of Early Settlers in Trenton and Ewing*, p. 120. Polly's husband was Benjamin Hendrickson, Eliza Hill's uncle.

168. Ibid., pp. 121–122. Elijah Hendrickson married Randolph Hunt's sister, Louisa. Reuben Hendrickson married Isabella Lanning.

169. United States Federal Census Year: *1840*; Census Place: *Ewing, Mercer, New Jersey*; Roll: *254*; Page: *104*; Image: *214*; Family History Library Film: *0016518*. Daniel Hart lived next door to John Hendrickson in Ewing.

170. Hill, "Descendants of Paul Hill and Rachel Stout," p. 4. John Hazard married Eliza Hill's sister, Joanna.

171. Deats, *Marriage Records of Hunterdon County*, p. 125. Charles Smith married Elizabeth Hazard 27 September 1838.

172. Cooley and Cooley, *Genealogy of Early Settlers in Trenton and Ewing*, p. 275; Deats, ibid., p. 131. Enos Titus (1768–1840) was an elder of the Pennington Methodist Church. He married Elizabeth Hill, Jediah's cousin, the daughter of Jediah's uncle James and his wife, Rachel Coles Hill. Elizabeth was a sister of Samuel C. Hill.

173. Phyllis B. D'Autrechy. *An Historical and Genealogical Record of the First United Methodist Church of Pennington, 1774–1974, Pennington, New Jersey* (Trenton, NJ: Trenton Printing Co., 1984), pp. 67, 76–77. Maria Titus (1804–1886) married Joseph Bunn in 1824. He was an undertaker and founder of a seminary for young ladies, later known as Lasher's Seminary. Maria and Joseph are buried in the Old Methodist Cemetery, Pennington, New Jersey.

174. Wikipedia, "Threshing Machine," last modified August 14, 2011; http://en.wikipedia.org/wiki/Threshing_machine.

175. Deats, *Marriage Records of Hunterdon County, New Jersey*, p. 116. Sarah Boggs, born 1 August 1789, married John R. Hageman on 7 November 1810. The full identity of the mentioned sister-in-law is unknown.

176. Otley and Keily, *Map of Mercer County, New Jersey*. John Hageman resided in Ewing Township, New Jersey.

177. *The African Repository*, Volume 14 for 1838, No. 1, January 1838, p. 194. Reverend M. J. Reese was listed as a delegate to the State Colonization Convention in Trenton, New Jersey, on July 10, 1838. Among the business conducted at that Convention was a resolution: "That the object of the Society shall be to circulate information among the inhabitants of this State . . . and secure for the people of color, in New Jersey, if they prefer it, a distinct settlement in Liberia, under the control of the American Colonization Society."

178. Joseph M. Wilson, *Presbyterian Historical Almanac & Annual Remembrancer of the Church, for 1861*. (Philadelphia, PA: Joseph M. Wilson, 111 South

Tenth Street, below Chestnut Street, 1861), p. 224. This may have been Reverend James M. Willson. Reverend Willson was Moderator of the Synod of the Reformed Presbyterian Church and a professor at the Theological Seminary in Allegheny, Pennsylvania, as well as Chairman of the Board of Domestic Missions and Publisher of *The Covenanter*, a monthly periodical published in Philadelphia.

179. James P. Snell, assisted by Franklin Ellis and a Numerous Corps of Writers, *History of Hunterdon and Somerset Counties, New Jersey* (Philadelphia, PA: Everts and Peck, 1881), p. 93. Reverend William Pollard, born in 1783, was pastor of Wertsville Baptist Church in 1836. "In much bodily weakness and infirmity he served faithfully three years, dying November 30, 1839, much beloved. He baptized twenty-one persons during his pastorate."

180. John Warner Barber and Henry Howe, *Historical Collections of the State of New Jersey* (New York, NY: Published for the Authors by S. Tuttle, 194 Chatham-Square, 1844), p. 253. Reverend Charles Bartolette, born about 1784, died 15 December 1852. He was called as pastor to the Baptist Church in Flemington, New Jersey, in 1812. Members from this church were "set off" to form the Wertsville Baptist Church.

181. No information has been found about Reverend George.

182. United States Federal Census Year: *1830*; Census Place: *Amwell, Hunterdon, New Jersey*; NARA Roll: *M19- 83*; Page: *324*; Family History Film: *0337936*. William Young, a miller, lived near Peter Wilson in Amwell. This may be the residence Henry visited.

183. United States Federal Census Year: *1850*; Census Place: *North Brunswick, Middlesex, New Jersey*; Roll: *M432_455*; Page: *290B*; Image: *590*. Possibly Isaac Stout, a cabinetmaker. The Hill family was related to the Stouts, but the exact connection to Isaac Stout is unknown.

184. Thomas Longworth, *Longworth's American Almanac, New-York Register and City Directory for 1839* (New York, NY: 118 Nassau Street, 1839), p. 654. James H. Townsend, a dry goods merchant, is listed at 707 Greenwich Street.

185. Bear's Mill online, "History of the Mill," accessed January 12, 2012; *www.bearsmill.com/history.html*.

186. Norris F. Schneider, *The National Road: Main Street of America* (Columbus, OH: Ohio Historical Society, 1975), p. 22.

187. Eric Sloane, "The Mills of Early America," *American Heritage*, Volume 6, No. 6, October 1955, p. 105.

188. David Larkin, *Mill: The History and Future of Naturally Powered Buildings* (New York, NY: Universe Publishing, 2000), pp. 15–16.

189. Ibid., p. 11.

190. Ibid., p. 16.

191. Wikipedia, "Second Bank of the United States," last modified January 11, 2012; *www.wikipedia.org/wiki/Second_Bank_of_the_United_States*.

192. Michael F. Holt, *The Rise and Fall of the American Whig Party: Jacksonian Politics and the Onset of the Civil War* (New York, NY: Oxford University Press, 1999), p. 105.

193. Ibid., p. 61.

194. Wikipedia, "Second Bank of the United States," op.cit.

195. Murray Rothbard, *A History of Money and Banking in the United States: The Colonial Era to World War II*. Edited with an Introduction by Joseph T. Salerno. (Auburn, AL: The Ludwig Von Mises Institute, 2002), pp. 95–99.

196. Holt, *Rise and Fall of the American Whig Party*, p. 105.

197. Schneider, *The National Road: Main Street of America*, p. 24.

198. Vivian, *A Driving Tour of the National Road in Pennsylvania*, p. 4.

199. Thompson,, *The National Road*, p. 104.

200. Schneider, *The National Road: Main Street of America*, p. 4.

201. Thompson, *The National Road*, p. 172.

202. Ibid., p. 117.

203. Schneider, *The National Road: Main Street of America*, pp. 9–10.

204. Ibid., p. 15.

Endnotes for Prologue and Section I

205. Ibid., p. 15.

206. Harry Sinclair Drago, *Canal Days in America: The History and Romance of Old Towpaths and Waters.* (New York, NY: Clarkson N. Potter, Inc., 1972), p.222.

207. Ohio Department of National Resources online, "History of Ohio Canals," accessed January 17, 2012, http://ohiodnr.com/water/canals/canlhist/tabid/3285/Default.aspx.

208. Ohio Hiking Trails: Miami and Erie Canal online, "Miami and Erie Canal History," accessed January 12, 2012; *http://www.hiking.ohiotrail.com/trails/canal-history.htm.*

209. Drago, *Canal Days in America*, p. 219.

210. "History of Ohio Canals," op. cit.

211. U. S. History online, "An Explosion of New Thought: Prison and Asylum Reform," accessced February 16, 2012, at *www.ushistory.org/us/26d.asp.*

212. Cayuga County Historian online, "Early History of Cayuga County — Auburn Prison," accessed February 16, 2012, at *www.co.cayuga.ny.us/history/cayugahistory/prison.html.*

213. Howe, *Historical Collections of Ohio*, p. 642.

214. Howe, *Historical Collections of Ohio*, pp. 645–646.

215. Medary, *Columbus Business Directory, for 1843–4*, pp. 104–105.

216. Howe, *Historical Collections of Ohio*, p. 645.

217. Ibid.

218. Archer Taylor, "Number Six." *Western Folklore*, 22 (1963) pp. 193–194, accessed January 12, 2012; *www.folkmed.ucla.edu.*

219. Felter, *King's American Dispensatory*, accessed January 12, 2012; *www.henriettesherbal.com/eclectic/kings/index.html.*

220. Felter, *King's American Dispensatory.*

221. George P. Wood, M.D., and E. H. Murdock, M.D., Ph.D. *Vitalogy, or Encyclopedia of Health & Home Adapted for Home and Family Use.* (Chicago, IL: I. N. Reed, M.A. Donohue & Co., Printers and Binders, 1904) p. 603.

222. UCLA Folklore Archives, accessed January 12, 2012; *www.folkmed.ucla.edu.*

223. Wood, *Vitalogy*, p. 505.

224. Revolutionary Soldiers Monument, Pennsylvania online, "Revolutionary Soldiers Cemetery," accessed September 24, 2011, *www.eastvincent.org.*

225. Texian Legacy Association online, "TLA Lady's Page: Starting Out: Women's Clothing — 1830s Style," accessed January 12, 2012; *www.texianlegacy.com/ladys.html.*

226. Conner Prairie Interactive History Park online, "Clothing of the 1830s," accessed January 12, 2012; *http://www.connerprairie.org/Learn-And-Do/Indiana-History/America-1800-1860/Clothing-of-the-1830s.aspx.*

227. Ibid.

228. Ibid.

229. Wikipedia, "Fulling" last modified on December 30, 2011; *http://en.wikipedia.org/wiki/Fulling.*

230. Wikipedia, "Ebeneezer Butterick," last modified on January 17, 2011; *http://en.wikipedia.org/wiki/Ebenezer_Butterick.*

231. Coletta, ed., *United States Navy and Marine Corps Bases, Domestic*, p. 477.

232. US Department of the Navy — Naval Historical Center Online Library of U.S. Navy Ships, accessed January 12, 2012; *www.history.navy.mil/photos/sh-usn/usnsh-p/penna.htm.*

233. Robin Moore, *The USS Preble, Sloop of War 1838–1863,* accessed January 21, 2012; *www.tfoenander.com/preble.htm.*

234. This letter was sold in an online auction in 2011. The link is no longer available.

235. Navy Department, Office of the Chief of Naval Operations. *Dictionary of American Naval Fighting Ships, Volume II* (Washington, DC: Naval History Division, 1963), p. 233.

Section II

2003–2009

Following in Henry's Footsteps

The typewritten copy of Henry's journal is twenty-one pages, single-spaced. Before I started to write this book, the notes and photocopies from my research filled two drawers in a filing cabinet. The background research was necessary for me to better understand Henry and his world, but once I decided to actually travel the route he had taken from Mount Pleasant to New York City, I hoped I would feel a deeper connection to Henry himself. That ever-growing connection between me and Henry and the places that had inspired his journal would become the heart of my quest.

Keri and I began our journey at the Hill/Rogers homestead on Covered Bridge Road on August 18, 2003, just as Henry and his family had done 165 years before. I wished I could have known what kind of preparations they had made before they left, as they were embarking on a four-month journey and would need both summer and winter clothing. I wondered if they worried about leaving their farm and mill to be run by the hired help for such a long time, and I wondered if I'd be able to experience some places along the route the way that Henry had seen them. I hoped so!

We walked through the quiet neighborhood where newer homes surround the old farmhouse. I pointed out the site of the mill to Keri. We walked across the covered bridge, and even knocked on the door of the farmhouse, but no one was home. Then we returned to the car, set the trip odometer on zero, and began our journey.

I had grown up in suburban Cincinnati, and I knew my way through Springdale and West Chester. I wanted to be true to Henry's experience, but Henry, of course, had not elaborated on his actual route out of town. I drove north on US Route 127 (Hamilton Road) to Springdale Road, then to Winton Road and Kemper Road through old Springdale. I picked up US Route 42 through part of West Chester. Union Village no longer appears on the road map, but a nearby shopping center is called Union Station. We continued north on US Route 42 and stopped in Lebanon for some antique shopping. Lebanon has a delightful downtown district, and is home of the Golden Lamb, a tavern that dates to 1803, and has been visited by twelve United States Presidents, Mark Twain, and Charles Dickens. I love the Golden Lamb. When I was a kid, it

Figure 73. The Golden Lamb Inn has been a fixture in Lebanon, Ohio, since 1803.

was a special treat to eat there when my dad's aunt and uncle visited from Florida.

Keri and I took State Route 48 to Centerville and drove through the suburbs near Dayton. The Hills and the Rogers had traveled this road to visit family and friends in Miami County. We stopped at the Miami County Courthouse in Troy to look at land records, but alas! I found no 19th-Century county maps on file, an early disappointment that foiled my plan to locate and stand on my ancestors' land.

We left the courthouse with no new information, except maybe the knowledge that field research was going to be harder and perhaps less productive than I'd thought. We made the short trip north to Fletcher, where we explored the cemetery and found the city lot where Charlotte Duer's house once stood. We then continued east on State Route 36, through Lena (formerly known as Elizabethtown), Saint Paris, and Westville to Urbana. From Urbana, we took State Route 29 to Mechanicsburg. Henry had complained that there was no place to stop for eighteen miles along this stretch of road, and nothing much had changed in that respect. Keri and I then came to West Jefferson, where the family stopped to spend their first of fifteen nights in taverns before they were joyfully received by their New Jersey relatives. We had much more travel ahead of us that day, and we continued into Columbus, where we stopped at home. We would continue on our journey the next day.

In Henry's time, the National Road entered Columbus on Broad Street, jogged south on High Street, then continued east on Main Street. Nowadays, US Route 40 jogs south on Drexel Avenue in Bexley, the suburb where we live. There is one National Road marker in Bexley, on Main Street, at Christ Lutheran Church.

On our second day, Keri and I drove through Bexley's shopping district, past the public library and the bronze historical marker commemorating the National Road, and continued traveling east. The landscape had a distinctly suburban flavor for the next ten miles or so. Hibernia, though it's no longer there, has a namesake — an apartment complex near Big Walnut Creek. A friend who worked at the Ohio Historical Center told me there is a settlers' cemetery among the trees above the creek.

Figure 74. This abandoned bridge on Old National Road, west of Zanesville, stands in sharp contrast to the preserved S Bridge at Fox Run shown in figures 79 and 80.

Figure 75. The same abandoned bridge viewed from the side.

Next was Reynoldsburg, which may have swallowed Havana — I couldn't really be sure. My 1830s map of Ohio did not show either Havana or Reynoldsburg.

In Etna, a side street named Toll Gate Road stood as a reminder of the past. After Kirkersville, we left the suburbs behind and passed into more rural areas, Luray and Hebron first. Hebron had a bronze historical marker describing how the Ohio and Erie Canal and the National Road had intersected in Hebron, and the canal bed near the road was still evident. Hebron was a brisk center of commerce during Henry's era. The legacy continues for this quiet village along the National Road — less than a mile north of the old center of town, a large industrial park is home to corporations like Diebold and Harry & David.

Jacksontown, Linville, Gratiot, and Hopewell were little crossroad towns on US Route 40, which runs parallel to today's Interstate 70. I preferred traveling on the state route. There were interesting things to see and the slower pace allowed us to stop frequently, instead of just whizzing by as we would have done had we been driving on the expressway.

Just before lunch we drove past a large stone house nestled in a curve of the road a few miles west of Zanesville. Henry

Figure 76. The Smith House Tavern in Mount Sterling, Ohio. In 1838, Edward Smith was the proprietor. Later, the tavern was owned by Edward's son Alexander.

had written in his journal that the family arrived in Mount Sterling about sunset and "put up at Mr. Smith's exchange, where we were tolerably entertained." I looked over my shoulder and said out loud, "Hey — wait a minute!" and turned the car around to check it out. Sure enough, "Smith" was spelled out in the roof tiles of an outbuilding and a sign out front said "Historic Smith House Antiques and Collectibles." The cornerstone on the building read 1830. This was a notable and unexpected discovery!

Smith House Antiques is my favorite kind of antique store — where I can dig around and have an impromptu treasure hunt. The main floor had a circular flow, and I wandered into a chilly back hallway. The chill persisted as I returned to the main room. Judith Lowther, the owner, was behind the counter, near the front door. I sensed someone behind me, but when I looked, no one was there. We were the only customers, and Keri was interested in china figurines across the room. I asked, "Is it my imagination, or is someone following me?" Judith replied cheerfully, "Oh, it's probably the ghost. I think it's one of the Smith sisters." The tavern was so old, and Judith so offhand about it, that I readily accepted her belief in the ghost!

I introduced myself and told Judith about our quest to gather information about the places Henry mentioned in his journal. She kindly conducted us upstairs to see the tavern's original sleeping room on the second floor. The large room

Figure 77. Smith House Tavern outbuilding, which was not on the premises at the time of Henry's visit.

had been filled with beds during the house's tavern days, and it was there Henry and his family had most likely spent the night.

After we left the Smith House, Keri and I stopped at a Wendy's for lunch. When Henry and his family stopped at a tavern, they may have had limited menu items from which to choose. We had a much wider variety of restaurants open to us, but we chose quick meals most of the time. We then crossed the famous Y Bridge into Zanesville and proceeded to the Muskingum County Courthouse.

Here again, I was disappointed by my unproductive field research. Discovering the Smith House led me to set impossible standards to achieve my research goals. The time pressure unnerved me; I had hoped the information I sought would be out in the open (or at least carefully indexed) and I'd find connections to Henry everywhere — well, almost everywhere — I looked, but the opposite turned out to be true. We could not locate any information about the C & T Rogers Hotel mentioned in the journal, and there were no longer any mills on the riverbanks.

Figure 78. The Y Bridge as it appears today spanning the juncture of the Licking and Muskingum rivers in Zanesville, Ohio.

Currently there are four antique stores in downtown Zanesville, and six more east of the city on the National Road. If you're shopping for art pottery, this is Mecca. I was reluctant to stop and explore the shops on this trip because I knew I would fall too far behind schedule, but I've been back to shop many times since.

As we made our way east through Muskingum County, we came upon a stone S bridge off to the north side of the road and stopped to get a good look. This S Bridge, built in 1828, is curved at its approaches to maintain the direction of the road and yet to allow for the arch of the bridge to be built so that it was perpendicular to the creek it was crossing.

When we got out of the car to take pictures on the S bridge, we met Liz and Bob, who were sweeping and cleaning, spiffing things up for the Ohio Bicentennial Wagon Train, which was expected to arrive the next day. We told them of our mission, and at their urging read aloud Henry's journal entry about the Zanesville area. They showed us that if you sit in the shady grove above the S bridge, and look to the south, you can see

Figure 79. S Bridge Park, New Concord, Ohio, where the National Road crossed Fox Run Creek.

Figure 80. Fox Run Bridge at S Bridge Park, New Concord, Ohio, viewed from the side.

evidence of five different roadways: Zane's Trace, the old National Road, US Route 40, the railroad, and Interstate 70.

When construction detoured us onto Interstate 70 east of Zanesville, it felt strange trying to mark Henry's way on a modern expressway. The white mile markers on the National Road were like friendly sentinels, assuring me I was on the right track. I ditched the expressway as soon as I could, but US Route 40 merged with Interstate 70 again for a stretch east of Old Washington, and since I didn't realize there was an "old" section of the National Road, we ended up back on the expressway again and missed Middletown, Elizabethtown, Fairview, and Hendrysburg. Though we passed through Fairview on our return trip, I did not find evidence of William Armstrong's tavern. Another detail I'd hoped to confirm was, apparently, lost to the ages.

We finally got back on US Route 40 at Morristown, and as we got closer to West Virginia, the road twisted and wound over and under the expressway. I agreed with Henry that this road was "crooked as a black snake." Keri and I crossed into West Virginia at Bridgeport, Ohio, on the suspension bridge with the expressway travelers. In the ten-mile-wide stretch of West Virginia over which we traveled, we were up hill and down dale.

Henry called the landscape in what was then Virginia "the most hilly country ever I saw." Of course, that was before he got to the mountains along the Pennsylvania/Maryland border!

Those mountains are monsters — they go up, up, up and then down with curves and grades of up to 13%. Keri said she'd rather walk than try to drive a wagon on those roads, and I agreed — I couldn't imagine trying to urge a team of horses up, much less control them on the way down! Travelers on the National Road sometimes cut down trees and dragged them behind their wagons on steep downgrades. Cut saplings could augment wagon brakes if one jammed them in next to the wheels to create more friction.

We stopped in Scenery Hill, Pennsylvania, to check out an "historic inn and tavern" for sale. The building was serving as an antique store, and was in a state of considerable disrepair. I rarely pass up an antique store, but when I saw the hand-lettered signs on the screen door, I wasn't too disappointed the store was closed. "Only ill-mannered people are allowed to slam the door." "We are here to sell, not to entertain you." "You Break It You Bought It." Charming . . .

Around West Brownsville, where US Route 40 crosses the Monongahela River, I lost track of the National Road, and we ended up in California, Pennsylvania, about five miles upriver. I have no idea what I did to cause our unexpected detour, but Keri read the map and got us back on track.

We stopped for a relaxing sit-down dinner on Chalk Hill at the beautifully restored Stone House Tavern. This section of the National Road was familiar, so we didn't need to make discoveries. I felt a happy, homecoming kind of sensation when we drove through Addison where, a few months earlier, I had

Figure 81. Keri took this picture of me at the Stone House Tavern.

Figure 82. The Stone House Tavern on Chalk Hill is a beautifully restored restaurant and inn.

Fips, Bots, Doggeries, and More

Figure 83. The Augustine House, Addison, Pennsylvania.

decided to drive the road myself and tell my story along with Henry's. The pull of the past is very strong for me there.

Once we crossed the Maryland state line, the press was on to find a hotel. Many chain hotels locate near expressway exits, but on US Route 40, our choices were few. Henry mentioned stopping at three taverns between Cumberland and Flintstone before they found an acceptable choice. I wished I had three choices after I missed the turnoff for a Holiday Inn in Cumberland, but I saw no other hotels until we reached Hancock, 35 miles farther east, and by then it was dark. We found a motel but no pool, which was a disappointment for Keri, but it was a place to stay. So far, we had logged 450 miles from Mount Healthy, Ohio, to Hancock, Maryland.

Henry's trip included visits to family, and happily, so did ours. We spent a day and a half visiting with my sister, Kim, and her family in Towson, Maryland. We enjoyed seeing their new home, and had a busy day at Inner Harbor, where we took the girls to Fort McHenry, rode paddleboats, and helped bring up the anchor on the USS *Constellation*. This, the second USS *Constellation*, was constructed at the Norfolk Navy Yard in 1854. This ship, completely restored in 1999, was reconfigured to resemble the original frigate *Constellation* (1797–1853), and is open to the public. By touring this ship, I was able to imagine the frigate *Dale*, which Henry and his family saw at the Philadelphia Navy Yard.

The next day, Keri and I drove to Hagerstown, Maryland. We found a room, and a pool, at the Sleep Inn there. After dinner, we went shopping at a nearby outlet mall, got ice cream, then went back to the hotel and had a swim. Shopping

Figure 84. The Addison Craft Shop, Addison, Pennsylvania.

Figure 85. Keri and her cousin Alex Pearson on an anchor at Fells Point, Maryland.

was the perfect way to wrap up our day on the road. I enjoyed looking at the changing landscapes as much as Henry did, but I was also happy to see a Gap outlet store on the horizon! Before bed, I looked over my notes and prepared for a visit to the Washington County Historical Society. Total miles so far — 650.

The next morning we ate breakfast at Cracker Barrel and set out for the Historical Society, where we met with Mindy, who located the Rising Sun Tavern on a city map from the mid-19th Century. The Washington County Free Library currently occupies the site. Next, she helped us locate a tavern in Leitersburg, Maryland, which was owned by John Lahm. Mindy recommended we go off-route to Lehman's Mill, which had been in operation from 1770 until about 1999, and is now a gift shop and antique store. We made the lovely drive out Maryland Route 60, and drove past fields of cows, rocks, and goats. I stopped to photograph the field of protruding rocks, because it was exactly like Henry's description of the area.

Figure 86. Alex, Keri and I await orders to bring up the anchor on the USS *Constellation*.

Lehman's Mill is located in a lovely rural setting. There is a farmhouse next door, ducks in the old mill tail, and cows in the pasture. The shop's owner took us to the basement to show us the old gears that turned with the water wheel. We bought some souvenirs and chatted with the ladies who ran the shop. They assured me that many taverns on the way to York are still standing. To cap things off, we drove to the tiny crossroads town of Leitersburg, the predetermined spot at which I would end this segment of our journey. It was hard to stop, but we had to get back to our daily lives.

Figure 87. Stanton's Mill, built 1859, Grantsville, Maryland. The mill is located on the National Road, in the Penn Alps artisan village, and is open to the public.

Figure 88. Keri with millstone at Stanton's Mill, Grantsville, Maryland. This millstone is cut in the wagon wheel pattern.

So Keri and I headed west on US Route 40, through Clear Spring and Indian Spring. Shortly after we passed over Sideling Hill, I made a wrong turn, left US Route 40, and got lost. Though frustrating, making a wrong turn didn't take a toll on us as it did on "man and horse" in Henry's time. He lamented over going a mile in the wrong direction.

In Grantsville, Maryland, near Casselman's Bridge, we spent some time at Stanton's Mill and an antique store. Keri bought some Wade porcelain figurines for her collection, and I bought some cornmeal ground at the mill. The mill, recently restored, provided us with a great opportunity to see a water-powered mill in operation, even if it wasn't one of the mills Henry mentioned in the journal.

At Washington, Pennsylvania, we stopped at the Ramada Inn. I asked for a non-smoking room, but got one that wasn't. The odor gave me a headache, and I was glad to leave the room and get pizza for dinner. It was still light out when we finished eating, and, to delay our return to the room, Keri and I raced each other across the hotel grounds, then strolled around the parking lot. Antique car enthusiasts were setting up for a cruise-in, so we walked up and down the rows, looking at the cars. We were at the far end of the parking lot when a shabby-looking man tried to get my attention. At first, I thought he was talking to someone else. After a few seconds, he seemed to realize we didn't know each other, but kept advancing, and said I looked like someone "from the mission."

I tried to freeze him with "I don't think I know you," and stepped around him, keeping Keri by the hand. The man followed us, apologizing. By this time I was pretty sure he was drunk, so I turned and said pointedly, "That's ok — just leave us alone," then kept walking toward the hotel. The hotel manager held the door open for us, and as we went inside, asked if the man was bothering us. I realized the manager was in the doorway keeping an eye on the strange man, but I said, "I think it was just an honest mistake," took Keri upstairs, and locked us in to our smelly used-to-be-a-smoking room.

Keri watched the Disney channel that evening while I got organized for the trip home. Total miles so far — 841.

I got up about 7:00 A.M. and finished packing. Keri was buried under her covers, but when I said, "Time to get up — we're going home today!" I got a smile before she pulled the covers back over her head.

We had breakfast in the hotel dining room and were on the road by 8:30. In Wheeling we stopped to photograph the Madonna of the Trail statue, one of twelve erected by the Daughters of the American Revolution across the country on US Route 40 and US Route 66, to honor female pioneers. We

Figure 89. Madonna of the Trail statue, Wheeling, West Virginia.

115

Figure 90. Keri at the Ohio Bicentennial Wagon Train campsite.

Figure 91. The Wagon Train traveled at a pace commensurate with Henry's. They averaged 12 miles a day.

Figure 92. Keri at Bexley's National Road marker, the official end of our first journey.

scouted the exact location of the Sign of the Wagon tavern at the corner of Main and 9th streets, but a couple of turns around the block led us to conclude that the tavern once stood where the road had been widened. As we crossed into Ohio, Keri cheered in the back seat.

We came upon the Ohio Bicentennial Wagon Train at the National Road/Zane Gray Museum near New Concord, so we stopped and looked at the wagons, mules, and horses, and talked with some of the participants. The Wagon Train was making a 285-mile journey across Ohio. Of the 1,500 participants, only five were traveling the entire way. One was a teacher from Worthington, near Columbus, who planned to walk the whole way and keep a journal of his experience, and two of the others were women in their sixties. The wagon train traveled about 12 miles a day, for 24 days.

Keri and I concluded our trip in front of Bexley's National Road mile marker. After the ceremonial taking of pictures, we went home; our trip odometer registered 1,000 miles as we pulled into the garage. And so our first circuit was complete.

On the Road Again — 2004

After we got home from our trip in 2003, I put the journal away. Bob was on sabbatical from his job at Capital University for the 2003–2004 academic year, and was traveling a lot. We chose to homeschool Keri so we could spend more time together as a family. The school year flew by, and I never made time for my project, but I was determined to keep to my plan to drive the second part of the route in August. A couple weeks before we left, I dug out my files, hastily refamiliarized myself with the information we'd compiled the year before, and then read through Henry's later journal entries with a sense of mounting apprehension.

The eastern segment of the trip was unfamiliar territory to me. The long list of relatives and friends that Henry's party had visited in the Trenton and Philadelphia entries was off-putting, and I didn't even try to unsnarl the family relationships.

My insecurity, lack of preparation, and the usual time constraints led me to concentrate my efforts on eastern Pennsylvania and Philadelphia. Trenton would become the focus of yet another trip, one that I would make alone.

The morning of our departure, I woke up fairly late after attending my twentieth high school reunion the night before. Keri and I left Bexley about 1:00 P.M. and took the expressway across Ohio and West Virginia. A couple of hours into the trip, Bob called to ask about the reunion. I told him I'd had a great time, and had been out until nearly five in the morning. "Put Keri on the phone," he said.

I handed the phone to Keri, and she immediately started to laugh. "Mom — Daddy says you're grounded."

I chose the Pennsylvania Turnpike because it seemed the most direct way to get to Fairfield, Pennsylvania, the first town east of Leitersburg mentioned in Henry's journal. I regretted my choice — large trucks jockeyed for position in heavy traffic amid the chaos of road construction, and I drove white-knuckled all the way. We gratefully stopped for the evening at the Ramada Inn in Breezewood, Pennsylvania. Keri swam in the hotel pool, I unwound in the hot tub, and then we ordered room service and watched the Olympics on television. 288 miles today.

The next morning, we left the hotel at 8:30 A.M. Henry had turned north at Leitersburg, Maryland, and we cut southeast on US Route 30, the Lincoln Highway, to intersect with his route at Fairfield. The road was hilly, rural, and picturesque,

Figure 93. The Fairfield Inn in Fairfield, Pennsylvania.

with sunshine filtering through the fog hanging in the air. We cut down local roads through Cashtown, Ortanna and into Fairfield. The Fairfield Inn is a lovely three-story brick structure with a gallery-style front porch. Henry stopped at a tavern run by a J. Weigle, but did not mention the tavern's name. I wanted to get a look inside, just in case it was the right place, but the door was locked. I knocked, but the man who answered the door was a guest, and did not want to let us in to look around. We took some pictures of the outside then pressed on toward Gettysburg. I later determined that the tavern I sought was known as the Black Horse Tavern, which is now a private residence located just west of Gettysburg.

We did not find the Cross Keys Tavern when we drove through Gettysburg. Even in a town as steeped in history as Gettysburg, I had to work to find the details I sought! It was Sunday, and the historical society was closed, so further inquiry would have to wait. I wished we had time to stay in Gettysburg and be tourists for a couple days, but we were meeting my sister and her girls for lunch in York.

It took about fifteen minutes to find Kim, Alex, and Julia because we kept missing each other on York's one-way downtown streets. We finally parked the cars and set out on foot with our cell phones, laughing and asking, "Can you see me now?" Once we were reunited, we took the girls to McDonald's for lunch and then spent the afternoon at Nixon Park, where we looked through the Nature Center and took a walk in the woods. After passing a pleasant afternoon watching the girls

Figure 94. The Black Horse Tavern, built in 1812, served as a field hospital and temporary headquarters for Robert E. Lee during the Battle of Gettysburg. It is now a private residence.

Figure 95. Buildings in historic downtown York, Pennsylvania.

Figure 96. Keri, Alex, and Julia Pearson in York, Pennsylvania.

play, Kim and her girls headed back to Towson, and Keri and I pressed on to the east.

We passed through Columbia and Lancaster, then turned onto State Route 23 toward Norristown. At first I noted names of towns Henry had mentioned in the journal, but after Morgantown we went through a fifteen-mile stretch where none of the names were familiar, and I began to fear I was on the wrong road. Then, all of a sudden we passed a large white building, with "Historical 7 Stars 1736" painted on it in blue. The Seven Stars had been a public house for over two hundred fifty years, and currently is a four-star restaurant with a menu that boasted a variety of steaks and seafood.

About two miles east of the Seven Stars was the Revolutionary War Soldiers Cemetery — one of the first places I'd

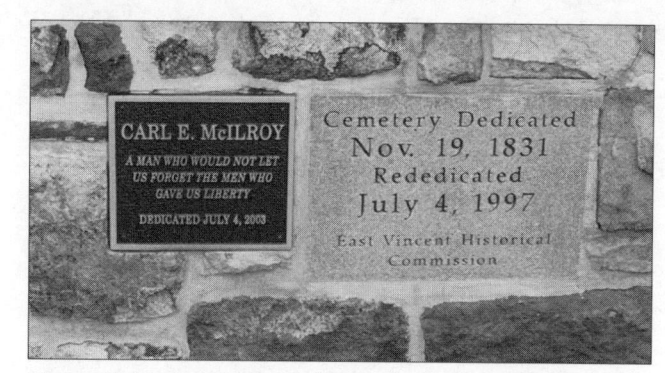

Figure 97. Dedication signs at the Revolutionary Soldiers Cemetery in East Vincent Township, Pennsylvania.

researched when I started to explore Henry's journal. In 1991, I had corresponded with Carl McIlroy, the first chairman of the East Vincent Township Historical Commission, who had used Henry's journal entry to raise local interest and spur efforts to preserve the cemetery; the wall around the cemetery had been repaired, and the site had been rededicated on July 4, 1997.

Late that afternoon, Keri and I stopped at Valley Forge. We saw the historical film and got to browse in the gift shop, and as we drove out through the park, Keri delighted in the herds of deer that had gathered in the dusk.

When we reached Norristown we were absolutely starving, and ate a huge dinner at an Italian restaurant. We were also very tired and, typically, we had trouble finding a hotel. We checked in to an Extended Stay America, where we collapsed on the beds and finished our very long day by watching the Olympics. Total miles so far: 478.

We decided to explore Philadelphia the next day, and when we arrived at the historic district, we parked the car and took a double-decker tour bus. The bus tour went past the wall at the Museum of Art that was part of the Fairmount Water Works, on which Henry remarked in his journal. After we rode once around the city, we got off the bus, toured the Betsy Ross House, found Ben Franklin's grave, and saw Independence Hall and the Liberty Bell. We had lunch in a food court across the street from Independence Hall, and later bought soft pretzels and Italian ices from street vendors.

On Tuesday, we traveled back to Lancaster, took a walking tour of the historic district, and saw where the Leopard Hotel once stood. We spent time at Lancaster County's Historical Society, where Keri helped me find documents about the history of the Leopard Hotel.

That afternoon, we took a room at a TraveLodge in Lancaster, which I can only describe as . . . "icky." It might have been nice about thirty years ago, and of course we ended up in a smoking room (again!) even though I specifically asked for non-smoking. The place was far from full, but all the empty rooms smelled of smoke. Things went from bad to worse: I selected a restaurant from the limited nearby choices that was more expensive than the other places we'd dined that week, and I paid way too much for an entree I didn't like. Keri's was edible, though, and I picked some food off her plate.

After dinner, we went to CVS and bought a hair dryer, because there wasn't one provided in the hotel room. I also got a snack. Then we went back to our stinky room and watched the Olympics. I was grumpy, and realized I'd had my fill of travel. I was glad to know we'd be home in two days. We had 581 miles behind us now.

We left Lancaster as early as possible, and traveled west with one goal left — to find Searight's Tavern, near Uniontown in southwestern Pennsylvania. The year before, I had taken photos of several buildings that might have been Searight's Tavern, and I needed help to figure out which one it was. Thomas B. Searight had been a newspaperman, local historian, and an elected official. He wrote the first detailed record of the National Road, entitled *The Old Pike*, in 1896. His book listed all the taverns and tavern keepers along the road, and I had used it so much in my research that I felt a photo of his tavern should be included in my records. It was several hours' drive back to western Pennsylvania, and when we arrived, we were ready to stretch our legs and find that tavern. First, we stopped at an antique store to ask if anyone there knew which was the Searight building, and Keri bought some more Wade figurines for her collection. At the clerk's recommendation, we drove over to an ancient service station to inquire further. The owner of the garage was a pretty crusty old guy, and, when I told him why I was there, he spent half an hour complaining about tourists and local history seekers. Only then did he tell us that Searight's tavern was the big pile of bricks across the road. It was disappointing to learn that the tavern had been demolished several years ago.

We left Uniontown, and almost immediately I made a wrong turn and ended up in the town of California — again! After Keri navigated us back onto US Route 40, we continued west and ate a late lunch in Washington, Pennsylvania. From there, we got back on the interstate and arrived home in time for dinner. Total miles on this trip — 982.

Back East — 2009

I flew to Philadelphia alone on May 1, 2009. I missed Keri, but I was determined to finish my field research and start writing. I had spent the better part of two months unraveling and identifying the cast-of-thousand-relatives in Trenton and scattered throughout Hunterdon County, New Jersey,

Figure 98. Soldiers' Barracks at Trenton, New Jersey. A paper mill was being excavated at the Petty's Run Archeological site, between the Barracks and the State House, during my visit in 2009.

and all that was left was for me to see the family's hometown for myself.

Upon arrival in Philadelphia, I rented a car and drove to Trenton. I stopped in at the downtown library's archives, ate dinner, and found a hotel room. The next morning, I drove north out of the city. I was armed with a road map, but I wanted to wander, and allowed myself to get lost every now and then.

I happened upon a sign for the New Jersey State History Fair, which was in progress at Washington Crossing State Park. When I saw the sign, I thought, "Do I know how to get there?" — and the answer was "Yes!" I had passed near the park on my wanderings that morning. I found the History Fair with no trouble, parked and began to explore. The first thing I saw

Figure 99. State House, Trenton, New Jersey.

Figure 100. Row houses in the historic Mill Hill district of Trenton, New Jersey.

Figure 101. I got to see the last few innings of a vintage base ball game at the New Jersey State History Fair at Washington Crossing Park.

drove on Old Ridge Road through the village of Coventryville. I continued west, basking in the pastoral scenes of East Vincent Township and thinking that this place was still exactly like Henry saw it in 1838 — but then I crested a hill and saw dozens of cookie cutter houses and a stand of condominiums spread across the valley. Apparently time does not stand still, after all!

The Broad Axe Tavern is a giant stone structure that has graced the corner of Butler Pike and Skippack Pike since 1751, and underwent a complete renovation in 2009. I had happened along on the day of the restaurant's grand opening party, and got a tour of the building.

made my heart swell with joy — a vintage base ball game was in progress! I hadn't seen a vintage game in almost a year, and happily settled myself on a bale of straw and watched the last few innings. It seemed like a good omen to have vintage base ball both at the beginning and at the end of my journey.

When the game was over, I wandered through the vendor and information booths. It was there I met Catherine Medich from the New Jersey State Archives, who said she'd be working on Monday and would help me obtain copies of 1849 maps of Hunterdon and Mercer counties.

On Sunday, I set off for Ambler, Pennsylvania, to find the Broad Axe Tavern. As I drove west from Valley Forge, I noticed "Old Ridge Road" on a street sign, turned up the hill and

Figure 102. Old Ridge Road, Coventryville, Pennsylvania.

Figure 103. Old Ridge Road, near Coventryville, Pennsylvania, retains the charm of an earlier time.

Monday morning, I went straight to the New Jersey State Archives, where Catherine copied the county maps for me. When I was finished there, I left New Jersey and headed west into Pennsylvania. That evening, I spread the maps out on the bed in my hotel room and spent a couple hours with a highlighter, marking the land that had belonged to Henry's family and friends. There were so many familiar names! The maps helped me make educated guesses about which mills Henry and Jediah visited and identify the roads the family traveled on as they visited from house to house.

After spending most of Monday driving across Pennsylvania alone, I happily crossed into Ohio from Wheeling, West Virginia, on Tuesday morning. I was 125 miles from Columbus, and I knew I'd be there in less than three hours. Henry and the family still had days of traveling to go when they crossed back into Ohio near the end of their journey. I could understand why Henry might have chosen to stop writing in the journal on the way back!

∼

I've always been disappointed that Henry's journal ends so abruptly, and frustrated by his allusion to a second volume. No one in my family knows if a second volume actually ever existed, or if, perhaps, Henry just got tired of detailing the family's journey at the halfway point.

If the family followed the same overland route home that they had taken to New York, they were probably on the road another five weeks and would have arrived back in Mount Pleasant in mid-November. It is also possible that they traveled by flatboat from Brownsville, Pennsylvania, located on the Monongahela River. Many settlers, eager to homestead in the west, floated from Brownsville to Pittsburgh on the Monongahela, and then continued southwest on the Ohio River. Henry and his family could have disembarked at Cincinnati and driven the twelve miles home to Mount Pleasant.

∼

Epilogue

The Legacy of the Journal

Henry Rogers' journal was his legacy to future generations, and I am now part of that legacy, too. We may come to think of the written word as disposable, and no wonder, since it only takes seconds to send and delete an email or text message. Henry's journal survived to be transcribed and distributed among his descendants more than 100 years after it was written. Though the original journal itself is missing, Henry's story will never be lost.

When Keri accompanied me on the two trips that followed Henry's route of travel, she too came to know his legacy in a new light and to grow from the experience. She proved to be a great navigator and research partner, and I hope she will remember our road trips fondly. Now, at sixteen, Keri is a fearless traveler, both in the United States and abroad. She reads maps and searches for answers and plans adventures. And she tells a great story.

As I sought details about Henry, I established ties with my father's aunts, Florence Rogers Rieck and Winona Rogers Brigode, and as a result, I am friends with my second cousin, LauraLee Brigode Jingo. I am pleased to share this story with my family — those I know and those I haven't met yet!

I would happily take on another project like this, but of course I would do some things differently, because research methods have changed dramatically in the past twenty years. I would not need to pay for long distance telephone calls, or travel to libraries and historical societies and search the card catalogs and the stacks, as I did back in the 1990s. Details that used to take months to discover are now just clicks away on the Internet. I would utilize digitized copies of out-of-print books now available online to do most of the research from home before I set out to travel in Henry's footsteps. I would keep more detailed records of the sources I used in my research so I wouldn't have to backtrack to confirm a fact or construct a bibliography.

And if I were driving the National Road again, I would eat at all the restaurants that were once taverns Henry mentioned in his journal!

Writing about Henry has led me to take on several other writing projects that tell other people's stories. A new path in my journey has opened up, and I can't wait to see where it will lead.

Reflections on the Research

Should you have a journal, letters, or other documents from an ancestor, I encourage you to embark on your own journey and see what you can discover. This is how I got started:

I studied Henry's journal in layers. First, I sought general information about things that were part of Henry's everyday life. For instance, he would have experience with milling and farming techniques. I also focused on topics he might have read about in the newspaper, like politics or the construction of canals and the National Road.

Next, I set about mapping his route and verifying the names of towns and the locations and proprietors of the many taverns Henry mentioned, which proved the journal was authentic.

Then I made a list of every person, place, and thing Henry mentioned in the journal, and conducted general Internet searches. For the most obscure details, I sent email inquiries to historical societies or libraries, in which I would explain the nature of my research, quote a portion of the journal, and ask specific questions of each source.

I preferred to send out a number of inquiries on a single day, then turn my attention to another topic, work on that topic until I got stuck, then go in another direction, bouncing back and filling in the details one by one. I preferred to cycle through the files this way, because I could work on many different leads while I waited for responses from outside sources.

Henry mentioned 60 relatives in his journal. Sometimes he called them "Aunt Deborah" or "Grandma Hendrickson," but more often he referred to them formally — Mrs. Levi Pinney, for instance, with whom they visited in Columbus, was Henry's youngest sister, Maria.

I found Maria's identity in two different sources. *History of Hamilton County, Ohio with illustrations and biographical sketches,* by Henry A. Ford, A. M., and Kate B. Ford, included a biography of Henry Rogers, Sr., that listed his children and their spouses. In that entry, it stated that Maria Rogers married Levi Pinney, of Columbus.

Levi Pinney's family was listed in *History of the City of Columbus, Capital of Ohio, in Two Volumes,* by Alfred E. Lee, A. M. From this book, I learned that the Pinneys were a founding family of Worthington, Ohio, and Levi Pinney owned a blacksmith shop in Columbus.

I recommend using genealogy websites like Ancestry.com as a way to locate original sources. Family genealogies posted on the Ancestry.com website are not required to cite sources; inaccuracies can occur. Confirm all your details with two independent sources. I have an unpublished family history of the Hill family that is very accurate — but cites no references. I trust it completely, but nonetheless I find a second independent record to back up the details in that document.

Epilogue

Whenever possible, I suggest using Federal Census data to establish family relationships. Beginning with the 1850 Federal Census, the records include the name of each individual living in the household, as well as their ages and birthplaces.

I searched for many people, especially in New Jersey, so when I found one individual's name in census records, I checked several pages before and after that entry, and sometimes other names on my list were neighbors. I also looked at census records of ten, twenty, and even thirty years into the future for additional information about each individual, an effort which sometimes yielded interesting supplemental data, like which child inherited a parent's farm, who they married, the names of their children, and whether elderly grandmas and grandpas lived with their grown children's families.

One important way to know our past is through the words of the regular people who lived before us. I recall a passage from one of my favorite children's books — *Understood Betsy* by Dorothy Canfield. Betsy is a modern city child at the turn of the 20th Century who is unaccustomed to doing, or thinking, for herself. When her great aunt teaches her to make butter and tells Betsy that *she* had learned to make butter from her grandmother, who was born in 1776, Betsy muses. "Why! There were real people living when the Declaration of Independence was signed — real people, not just history people — old women teaching little girls how to do things — right in this very room, on this very floor — and the Declaration of Independence just signed!"

I have stood where Henry stood, and I know him through his words. I feel the connection to him, one of America's Real People.

Appendix I

Expenses

Henry recorded the cost of food, lodging, and other expenses the family incurred on their trip. This list includes all of the expenditures recorded in the journal, but this accounting is not complete. I noticed, for example, that he did not record the cost of the locksmith and the jeweler in Trenton or the cost of the women's dresses and bonnets.

$ 2.50	Supper/lodging/stable horses, Alvah Winchester Tavern, Jefferson, Ohio
0.875	5 admissions to prison in Columbus
2.25	Stable horses in Columbus, 2 nights
3.15	Tolls paid on National Road between West Jefferson and Mount Sterling, Ohio
2.00	Supper/lodging/stable horses, Smith Tavern, Mount Sterling, Ohio
0.315	Toll
1.26	Toll (4)
1.50	Breakfast at C & T Rogers Hotel, Zanesville, Ohio
0.25	Horse feed, noon
2.00	Supper/lodging/stable horses, Washington, Ohio
1.1875	Breakfast/horse feed, William Armstrong's Tavern, Fairview, Ohio
0.63	Toll (2)
0.25	Ferry to Wheeling Island, Virginia
0.375	Ferry to Wheeling, Virginia
1.26	Toll (4)
0.625	Horseshoes (2)
0.25	Barbershop shaves (2)
4.50	Supper/lodging/stable horses/breakfast, Captain Beymer's Tavern, Wheeling, Virginia
0.40	Toll (2)
0.315	Lunch in Claysville, Pennsylvania
2.125	Supper/lodging/stable horses, Pennsylvania Inn, Claysville, Pennsylvania
1.25	Breakfast at Upland House
0.375	Half-pint of Number 6 medicine
0.25	Toll bridge at Brownsville, Pennsylvania
0.5625	Toll (4)
3.875	Supper/lodging/stable horses/breakfast, Stoddard's Tavern on Keysers Ridge, Maryland

2.25	Supper/lodging/stable horses, Allegeny County, Maryland
1.25	Breakfast at Fletcher's Tavern, Flintstone, Maryland
0.125	Horseshoe
0.75	Toll
0.125	Toll
2.60	Supper/lodging/stable horses, Brosius' Tavern, Hancock, Maryland
1.25	Breakfast, Widow Bevins' Tavern
1.25	Blacksmith, tyres cut, Clear Spring, Maryland
1.00	Toll
0.13	Horseshoes (2)
2.00	Supper/lodging/stable horses, Rising Sun Tavern, Hagerstown, Maryland
1.25	Breakfast, Lahm's Tavern, Leitersburg, Maryland
2.125	Supper/lodging/stable horses Cross Keys Tavern, Gettysburg, Pennsylvania
1.315	Breakfast and horse feed, James Fink Tavern, Abbottstown, Pennsylvania
0.25	Horse feed, Peter Wilt Tavern, York, Pennsylvania
2.50	Supper/lodging/stable horses, Joshua Taylor Tavern, Pennsylvania
1.50	Breakfast/horse feed
0.75	Toll (2)
0.04	Toll
1.25	Breakfast, Morgantown, Pennsylvania
1.25	Breakfast/horse feed, Seven Stars Inn, East Vincent Township, Pennsylvania
0.125	Toll bridge
3.125	Supper/lodging/stable horses/breakfast Broad Axe Tavern, Norristown, Pennsylvania
0.25	Horse feed, Sign of the Bear, Richboro, Pennsylvania
0.065	Barbershop shave
0.875	Horseshoes
0.065	Barbershop shave
1.25	Supper/horse feed White Horse Tavern, Philadelphia, Pennsylvania
0.25	Horseshoes (2)
0.125	Horseshoe
1.25	Carriage fare
3.125	Railroad fare to New York City, New York

The costs listed above add up to $75.04. Using the Consumer Price Index to calculate the cost in 2010 dollars, $1 in 1838 would have been worth $24.20, making the cost of the one-way trip $1,815.96 in today's dollars.

Appendix II

Family Members Mentioned in the Journal

Henry mentioned many family members in his journal. Those members are listed here, along with an identification of their relation to the core family, their age at the time they are mentioned in the journal, the dates of their birth and death, and marriage information.

The Core Family

Jediah Hill, 45 (b. 26 Apr 1793, d. 4 Jul 1859); m. 29 Apr 1815 to **Eliza Hendrickson Hill, 41** (b. 31 Jan 1797, d. 21 Jun 1854)

Henry Rogers, 32 (b. 31 May 1806, d. 1 Dec 1896); m. 22 Sep 1832 to **Rachel Maria Rogers, 22** (b. 27 Jan 1816, d. 25 Apr 1888)

Other Family Members in order of their mention in the journal

William Anderson, 47 (b. 5 Sep 1790, d. 25 Oct 1874); m. to his second wife, Martha Hayhurst Smith, 32 (b. 1806, d. 1895)

> William was Eliza Hill's first cousin, the son of David Anderson, who was brother to Rachel Anderson Hendrickson. William was a physician in Warren County, Ohio.

J. Duer [Joshua Anderson Duer], 29 (b. 31 Jan 1809, d. 11 or 14 Apr 1889);
m. to Sarah Fryback, 24 (b. 28 Apr 1814, d. 23 Mar 1898)

> Joshua was Eliza Hill's first cousin, the son of Charlotte Anderson Duer, who was Rachel Anderson Hendrickson's sister.

Oliver Wharton, 31 (b. 17 May 1807, d. 25 Jan 1886); m. to Jane Duer, **34** (b. 16 Feb 1804, d. 11 Aug 1877)

Jane was another of Charlotte Duer's children, and Eliza Hill's first cousin.

Aunt Charlotte [Anderson Duer], 64 (b. 23 Jul 1774, d. 12 Jun 1861);
Widow of William Hollinshead Duer, (b. 14 Jan 1775, d. 26 Oct 1828)

Charlotte was Eliza Hill's aunt.

Enoch Drake, 37 (b. 27 Nov 1800, d.?); m. to Rachel Hendrickson, 34 (b. 15 Sep 1805, d. 1875)

Rachel was Eliza Hill's sister.

George Suber, 41 (b. 12 Nov 1796, d. 23 Sep 1860); m. to Elizabeth Duer, 37 (b. 18 Oct 1800, d. 8 Aug 1872)

Elizabeth was Eliza Hill's first cousin.

James Anderson, 65 (b. 1773, d. 1866); m. to his second wife, **Deborah Howell, 61** (b. 1777, d. 4 Apr 1852)

James Anderson was Charlotte Duer's brother, and Eliza Hill's uncle.

David Anderson, 67 (b. 17 Apr 1771, d. 22 Nov 1843); m. to Esther Hollinshead, 68 (b. 21 May 1770, d. 8 May 1856)

David was Charlotte Duer's brother, William Anderson's father, Eliza Hill's uncle.

Peter [Harvey Anderson], 37 (b. 1801, d. May 1869)
Joseph [DePuy Anderson], ?

David, 30 (b. 1808, d. ?)
Daniel Anderson, 18 (b. 1820, d. ?)

These four were sons of David Anderson and cousins to Eliza Hill.

George Worthington, 33 (b. 17 Feb 1815, d. 30 Jan 1886); m. to Esther Anderson Linton (widow), age 31, on 23 Oct 1837.

Esther was the daughter of David Anderson, and Eliza Hill's first cousin.

Ephriam Anderson, unknown.

James Anderson's son, Ephriam, reportedly died around 1832. The family connection for this Ephriam Anderson is uncertain.

Levi B. Pinney, 33 (b. 26 Nov. 1805, d. 4 Jun 1839); m. to **Maria Rogers Pinney, 28** (b. 1 Apr 1810, d. 6 Nov 1869)

Maria was Henry Rogers' youngest sister.

Hannah Burge, 22 (b. 1816, d. 1895)

Hannah was the daughter of Michael Burge and Sarah Rogers Burge, Henry's sister and brother-in-law.

John Hendrickson, 46 (b. 11 Mar 1793, d. 30 Sep 1864); m. to **Sarah Green Hendrickson, 44** (b. 14 Mar 1795, d. 28 Dec 1869)

John was Eliza Hill's brother.

Appendix II — Family Members

William Hendrickson, 37 (b. 26 Nov 1800, d. 21 Jan 1868); m. to **Rebecca Green Hendrickson, 34** (b. 1803, d. ?)

William was Eliza Hill's brother.

Asher Hill, 40 (b. 7 Jan 1798, d. Aug 1880); m. to **Margaret Green Hendrickson, 37,** his second wife, (b. 3 Jan 1801, d. 23 Feb 1865).

Asher was Jediah Hill's brother.

William Hendrickson, 17 (b. 1821, d.?)

William was John and Rebecca Hendrickson's son.

Randal Hunt, 44 (b. 1794, d.?); m. to **Martha Hendrickson Hunt, 30** (b. 17 Jan 1808, d.?)

Martha Hendrickson Hunt was Eliza Hill's youngest sister.

Israel Hendrickson, 35 (b. 20 Mar 1803, d. 27 Sep 1880); m. to **Eleanor Smith,** ?

Benjamin Stout Hill, 51 (b. 23 Sep 1787, d. 15 Apr 1844); m. to **Margaret Vandike Hill** (b. 1790, d. 1850)

Benjamin was known in documents as "Stout Hill."

David Hill (b. 1816, d. ?); m. to **Ann Sutphin** (b. 5 Sep 1819, d. 27 Dec 1881)
Jane Hill (b. 13 Feb 1813, d.?)
Juliet Ann Hill (b. 13 Apr 1818, d.?)

These three were Benjamin Stout Hill's children.

Samuel Coles Hill, 51 (b. 1787, d. ?)
m. to **Mary Higgins, 45** (b. 12 Aug 1793, d. ca. 1860)

Samuel was Jediah Hill's first cousin, son of his uncle James Hill.

Nathaniel Hill, 19 (b. 1819, d.?)
Charles Hill, 12 (b. 1826, d.?)

These two were Samuel Coles Hill's children

Hannah Hill, ?

No census records list Hannah as one of Samuel's children. It is possible she was married before the 1850 census was taken. We can assume she existed, for she is mentioned twice in the journal, during a visit to Samuel Hill's house, and also when the she accompanies the core family on their trip to New York.

Grandma [Rachel Anderson] Hendrickson, 70 (b. 27 Apr 1868, d. 14 Feb 1858)

Rachel was Eliza Hill's mother.

Isaac Dukemenere, 30 (b. ca. 1808, d. 7 Jan 1881); m. to Anne Duer Dukemenere, (b. 17 Aug 1807, d. 4 Sep 1866)

Anne was the daughter of Charlotte Anderson Duer. Isaac Dukemenere owned a store and farmlands in Fletcher, Ohio.

Patience Jones, 46 (b. 1792, d.?)

Patience was the daughter of Rachel Anderson Hendrickson's sister Mary, and Eliza Hill's first cousin.

Letitia Clossin Barwis, 22 (b. 1816, d?)

Letitia was Patience's half sister, and Eliza Hill's first cousin.

Mary "Polly" Stout Hendrickson, 57 (b. 1781, d.?)

Widow of Benjamin Hendrickson, Eliza Hill's uncle.

Mathilda
Elizabeth
Charity
Mercy
Frances Julia
Benjamin, 14 (b. 1824, d.?)

These six were children of Mary Stout Hendrickson.

Elijah Hendrickson, 60 (b. 1778, d. 7 Jul 1863); m. to **Louisa Hunt Hendrickson** (b. ?, d. ?)

Elijah was Rachel Anderson Hendrickson's brother-in-law.

Reuben Hendrickson, 45 (b. 1793, d. 29 Nov 1859); m. to **Isabella Lanning Hendrickson, 42** (b. 1796, d.?)

Reuben was Elijah Hendrickson's son, and Eliza Hill's first cousin.

John Hazard; m. to Johanna Hendrickson Hazard (b. 15 Sep 1805, d. 1875)

Johanna was Eliza Hill's sister.

Enos Titus, 70 (b. 1768, d. 1840); m. to Elizabeth Coles Hill

Elizabeth was the daughter of Jediah Hill's uncle James Hill, sister of Samuel C. Hill, and Jediah's first cousin.

Maria Bunn, 34 (b. 1804, d. 1886); m. to Joseph Bunn, 40 (b. 25 Jan 1798, d. 13 Dec 1854)

Maria was Jediah Hill's niece.

Appendix III

Credits for Photographs

Champaign Historical Museum 6

Hardwick, Kevin and Cindy 4

Lawson, Keri 81

Lawson, Tracy 1, 5, 9, 13, 14, 24, 25, 26, 27, 31, 32, 33, 34, 35, 41, 42, 43, 44, 45, 54, 55, 56, 57, 58, 59, 63, 67, 68, 69, 74, 75, 76, 77, 78, 79, 80, 82, 83, 84, 85, 87, 88, 89, 90, 91, 92, 93, 94, 95, 96, 97, 98, 99, 100, 101, 102, 103

Lowther, Judith 65

Muskingum County Historical Society 15, 16, 17, 19

Peterson-Emerick, Cherie 2

Prout, Don 3

Stone, Kim 86

Images in the Public Domain 7, 11, 12, 20, 36, 38, 49, 50, 60, 61, 62, 64, 70, 71, 72, 73

Images in author's private collection 8, 10, 18, 21, 22, 23, 28, 29, 30, 37, 39, 40, 46, 47, 48, 51, 52, 53, 66

Bibliography

The African Repository, Volume 14, No. 1. The American Colonization Society, January 1838.

Armstrong, J. R., and Samuel Medary, Printer. *Columbus Business Directory, for 1843–4*, 1843.

Barber, John Warner, and Henry Howe. *Historical Collections of the State of New Jersey.* New York, NY: Published for the Authors by S. Tuttle, 194 Chatham-Square, 1844.

Battle, J. H., ed. *History of Bucks County.* Spartanburg, SC: Reprint Co., 1985 (reprint of 1887 edition).

Beers, W. H. & Co. *The History of Miami County, Ohio: containing a history of the county, its cities, towns, etc….* Chicago, IL: W.H. Beers & Co., 1880.

Bell, Herbert C. *History of Leitersburg District, Washington County, MD….* Leitersburg, MD: Published by the author, 1898.

Breyfogle, William A. *Wagon Wheels; A Story of the National Road.* New York, NY: Aladdin Books, 1956.

Biddle, Clement. *The Philadelphia Directory.* Philadelphia, PA: Printed by James & Johnson, 1791.

Brown, Robert C. *The History of Madison County, Ohio….* Chicago, IL: W. H. Beers & Co., Publishers, 1883.

Bruce, Robert. *The National Road, Most historic Thoroughfare in the United States, and strategic eastern link in the National Old Trails Ocean-to-Ocean Highway.* Washington, DC or Old Slip, New York, NY: National Highways Association and the author, 1916.

Cist, Charles. *Sketches and Statistics of Cincinnati in 1851.* Cincinnati, OH: Wm. H. Moore & Co., Publishers, 1851.

Coletta, Paolo, E., ed. *United States Navy and Marine Corps Bases, Domestic.* Westport, CT: Greenwood Press, 1985.

Cooley, Eli F., and William S. Cooley. *Genealogy of Early Settlers in Trenton and Ewing "Old Hunterdon County," New Jersey.* Baltimore, MD: Genealogical Publishing Co., Inc., 1977.

Cromie, Alice. *Restored Towns & Historic Districts of America: A Tour Guide.* New York, NY: A Sunrise Book, E. P. Dutton, 1979.

"Cross Keys, New New Oxford, Was Site of Colonial Tavern Century and a Half Ago; Old Buildings Gone" *Gettysburg Times* (Gettysburg, PA), July 14, 1960.

Crumrine, Boyd, ed. *History of Washington County, Pennsylvania, with Biographical Sketches of Many of its Pioneers and Prominent Men.* Philadelphia, PA: L. H. Everts & Co., 1882.

D'Autrechy, Phyllis B. *An Historical and Genealogical Record of the First United Methodist Church of Pennington, 1774–1974, Pennington, NJ*. Trenton, NJ: Trenton Publishing Co., 1984.

Day, Sherman. *Historical Collections of the State of Pennsylvania*. Philadelphia, PA: George W. Gorton, Publisher, 1843.

Deats, Hiram E., ed. *Marriage Records of Hunterdon County, New Jersey 1795–1875*. Flemington, NJ: H. E. Deats, Publisher, 1918.

Drago, Harry Sinclair. *Canal Days in America: The History and Romance of Old Towpaths and Waters*. New York, NY: Clarkson N. Potter, Inc., 1972.

Earle, Alice Morse. *Stage Coach and Tavern Days*. New York, NY: The Macmillan Company, 1900.

Ege, Ralph. *Pioneers of Old Hopewell: With Sketches of Her Revolutionary Heroes*. Whitefish, MT: Kessinger Publishing, LLC, 2009 (reprint of 1908 edition).

Ellis, Franklin, and Samuel Evans. *History of Lancaster County, Pennsylvania*. Philadelphia, PA: Everts & Peck, 1883.

Felter, Harvey Wickes, M. D., and John Uri Lloyd, Phr. M., Ph.D. *King's American Dispensatory*. Cincinnati, OH: Ohio Valley Co., 1898.

Fess, Simeon D., ed. *Ohio: A Four-Volume Reference Library on the History of a Great State*. Chicago, IL: Lewis Publishing Co., 1937.

Ford, Henry A., A. M., and Mrs. Kate B. Ford. *History of Hamilton County, Ohio with Illustrations and Biographical Sketches*. Cleveland, OH: L. A. Williams & Co., Publishers, 1881.

Futhey, J. Smith, and Gilbert Cope. *History of Chester County, Pennsylvania, with Genealogical and Biographical Sketches*. Philadelphia, PA: Louis H. Everts, 1881.

Galbreath, Charles B. *History of Ohio Volume I*. Chicago, IL: The American Historical Society, Inc., 1925.

Gordon, Thomas F. *A Gazetteer of the State of New Jersey, 1834 Comprehending a General View of Its Physical and Moral Condition*. Trenton, NJ: Published by Daniel Fenton; John C. Clark, Printer, Philadelphia, PA, 1834.

Green, Jonathon. *Cassel's Dictionary of Slang: A Major New Edition of the Market-Leading Dictionary of Slang*. London, England: The Orion Publishing Group Ltd., 2005.

Greve, Charles Theodore, A.B., LL.B. *Centennial History of Cincinnati and Representative Citizens*. Chicago, IL: Biographical Publishing Co., 1904.

Harbaugh, Thomas, ed. *Centennial History Troy, Piqua and Miami County, Ohio*. Chicago, IL: Richmond-Arnold Publishing Co., 1909.

Harper, Glenn, and Doug Smith. *A Traveler's Guide to The Historic National Road in Ohio: The Road that Helped Build America*. Columbus, OH: Ohio Historical Society, 2005.

Harris, Maurine, and Glen Harris. *Ancestry's Concise Genealogical Dictionary*. Salt Lake City, UT: Ancestry Publishing, 1989.

Hill, Leonard, and Louise Hill. "Descendents of Paul Hill and Rachel Stout through Charles Hill, and of Moses Edwards and Desire Meeker through Uzal Edwards," Unpublished manuscript, 1953. Author's private collection.

Hill, N. N., Jr. *History of Licking County, Ohio, Its Past and Present*. Newark, OH: A. A. Graham & Co., 1881.

Holt, Michael F. *The Rise and Fall of the American Whig Party: Jacksonian Politics and the Onset of the Civil War*. New York, NY: Oxford University Press, 1999.

Bibliography

Howe, Henry, LL.D. *Historical Collections of Ohio in Two Volumes: An Encyclopedia of the State.* Cincinnati, OH: C. J. Krehbiel & Co., Printers and Binders, 1907.

Hulbert, Archer Butler. *Historic Highways of America, Volume 10: The Cumberland Road.* Cleveland, OH: The Arthur H. Clark Company, 1904.

Hunterdon County Cultural & Heritage Commission. *Vanishing Landscapes of Hunterdon County.* Flemington, NJ: Hunterdon County Cultural & Heritage Commission, 2003.

Ierley, Merritt. *Traveling the National Road: Across the Centuries on America's First Highway.* Woodstock, NY: Overlook Press, 1990.

Jackson, Joseph. *Market Street, Philadelphia: The Most Historic Highway in America, Its Merchants and its Story.* Philadelphia, PA: Public Ledger Co., 1914.

Johnson, Alan. "Reliving Ohio's Frontier." *Columbus Dispatch* (Columbus, OH), June 22, 2003.

Jordan, Philip B., and Jay Monaghan, ed. *The National Road.* Indianapolis, IN: The Bobbs-Merrill Co., 1948.

Juettner, Otto, A. M., M. D. *Daniel Drake and His Followers Historical and Biographical Sketches.* Cincinnati, OH: Harvey Publishing Co., 1909.

Kauffman, Vice Admiral James Laurence, U.S.N. *Philadelphia's Navy Yards 1801–1948.* The Newcomen Society of England American Branch, New York, NY: 1948.

Krumrine, Diane M. comp. "Index of Tavern License Applications Recommended and Granted for Taverns in What is Now Adams County, Pennsylvania, 1749–1899." Gettysburg, PA: Adams County Historical Society, 2004.

Lathrop, Elise. *Early American Inns and Taverns.* New York, NY: Arno Press. 1977.

Larkin, David, *Mill: The History and Future of Naturally Powered Buildings.* New York, NY: Universe Publishing, 2000.

Lee, Alfred E., A. M. *History of the City of Columbus, Capital of Ohio, in Two Volumes.* New York, NY, and Chicago, IL: Munsell & Co., 1892.

Lewis, Alice Blackwell. *Hopewell Valley Heritage.* Hopewell, NJ: The Hopewell Museum, 1973.

Map of Hagerstown, Washington County, Maryland. J. C. Sidney, Publisher, 1850.

Map of Hunterdon County, New Jersey, Entirely from Original Surveys by Samuel C. Cornell. Camden, NJ: Lloyd Van Der Veer and J. C. Cornell, Publishers, 1851.

Map of Mercer County, New Jersey, Entirely from Original Surveys by J. W. Otley and J. Keily, Surveyors. Camden, NJ: Lloyd Van Der Veer, Publisher, 1849.

Map of Miami County, OH, from Actual Surveys. William Arrott, C. E. Cincinnati, OH: S. H. Matthews, Publisher. Middleton, Strobridge & Co., Lithographers, 1858.

Martin, William T. *History of Franklin County: A Collection of Reminiscenses of the Early Settlement of the County; with Biographical Sketches, and a Complete History of the County to the Present Time.* Columbus, OH: Follett, Foster & Co., 1858.

McClellan, Elisabeth. *Historic Dress in America 1607–1870.* New York, NY: Benjamin Bloom, Inc., Publishers, 1904.

McClellan, Helen Maitland. "Old Mills and Their Builders," Unpublished paper presented to the Champaign County Historical Society, Urbana, Ohio, March 1938.

McCutcheon, Mark. *The Writer's Guide to Everyday Life in the 1800's*. Cincinnati, OH: Writer's Digest Books, 1993.

Mitchell, Sarah E. *Ladies' Clothing in the 1830's*. Chatham, VA: Mitchell Publications, 2005.

Moore, Joseph E., and R. Duff Green. *Thomas B. Searight's The Old Pike: An Illustrated Narrative of The National Road*. Orange, VA: Green Tree Press. 1971.

Navy Department, Office of the Chief of Naval Operations. *Dictionary of American Naval Fighting Ships, Volume II*. Washington, DC: Naval History Division, 1963.

Oberlin, Loriann Hoff. *The Everything American History Book*. Avon, MA: Adams Media Corporation, 2001.

Ohio Department of Geological Survey, Glacial Map of Ohio: Ohio Department of Natural Resources, Division of Geological Survey, 2005.

Old Northwest Genealogical Quarterly. Columbus, OH: Published by Old Northwest Genealogical Society, October 1903, p. 189.

Peterson, Arthur J., Chairman. Mount Healthy Sesquicentennial Celebration Committee. *Once Upon a Hilltop: Mount Healthy Area Sesqui-Centennial 1817–1967*.

Papers Read Before the Lancaster County Historical Society, Volume 23, No. 1, January 1919.

Prolix, Peregrine. *Journey Through Pennsylvania, 1835 by Canal, Rail and Stage Coach*. Philadelphia, PA: Grigg and Elliott, 1836.

Quirk, Katherine D. "Black Horse Tavern is former field hospital" *Gettysburg Times* (Gettysburg, PA) April 18, 1983.

Rothbard, Murray. *A History of Money and Banking in the United States: The Colonial Era to World War II*. Edited with an Introduction by Joseph T. Salerno. Auburn, AL: The Ludwig Von Mises Institute, 2002.

Schneider, Norris F. *The Famous Y Bridge at Zanesville, Ohio*. Zanesville, OH. 1958.

Schneider, Norris F. *The National Road: Main Street of America*. Columbus, OH: Ohio Historical Society, 1975.

Schneider, Norris F. *Y Bridge City: The Story of Zanesville and Muskingum County, Ohio*. Cleveland, OH: World Publishing Co., 1950.

Seabrook, Jack, and Lorraine Seabrook. *Images of America: Hopewell Valley*. Charleston, SC, Chicago, IL, Portsmouth, NH, San Francisco, CA: Arcadia Publishing, 2000.

Searight, Thomas B. *The Old Pike: A History of The National Road, with Incidents, Accidents and Anecdotes Thereon*. Uniontown, PA: Published by the author, 1894.

Silverstone, Paul H. *Warships of the Civil War Navies*. Annapolis, MD: Naval Institute Press, 1989.

Sloane, Eric. "The Mills of Early America," *American Heritage* Magazine, Volume 6, Number 6, October 1955.

Smith, Elmer L. *Grist Mills of Early America and Today*. Lebanon, PA: Applied Arts Publishers, 1978.

Stills, Samuel Harden. *Ohio Builds a Nation: A Memorial to the Pioneers and the Celebrated Sons of the "Buckeye" State*. Lower Salem, OH: The Arlendale Book House, 1939.

Sutor, J. Hope. *History Past and Present of the City of Zanesville & Muskingum County, Ohio*. Chicago, IL: S. J. Clarke Publishing Co., 1905.

Thompson, George F. and Karl Raitz, ed. *The National Road*. Baltimore, MD: Johns Hopkins University Press, 1996.

Bibliography

Trenton Historical Society. *A History of Trenton 1679–1929: Two Hundred and Fifty Years of a Notable Town with Links in Four Centuries.* Princeton, NJ: Princeton University Press, 1929.

Trestain, Eileen Jahnke. *Dating Fabrics: A Color Guide 1800–1960.* Paducah, KY: American Quilter's Society, 1998.

Vivian, Cassandra. *A Driving Tour of the National Road in Pennsylvania.* Monessen, PA: Trade Routes Enterprises. 1994.

Whitpain Township property tax records for 1838–9. On file at the Historical Society of Montgomery County, Pennsylvania.

Wilson, Sue Korn, and Kathleen Mulloy Tamarkin. *Images of America: Mt. Healthy*. Charleston, SC: Arcadia Publishing. 2008.

Wood, George P. M.D., and E.H. Murcock, M.D., Ph.D. *Vitalogy, or Encyclopedia of Health & Home Adapted for Home and Family Use.* Chicago, IL: I. N. Reed, M. A. Donohue & Co., Printers and Binders, 1904.

Writers' Program of the Work Projects Administration in the Commonwealth of Pennsylvania, *Pennsylvania: A Guide to the Keystone State.* New York, NY: Oxford University Press, 1940.

Websites and Web Pages

Answers.com.

Arnold, Beth. Tredyffrin Easttown Historical Society of Pennsylvania online, "Inns and Taverns," accessed September 28, 2011; http://www.tehistory.org/docs/DQ2007sample.pdf.

Atlantic Monthly online, August 1967, "Cincinnati," accessed September 25, 2011; http://www.wattpad.com/21871-the-atlantic-monthly-volume-20-no-118-august-1867?p=98.

Barefoot's World online, "John Hart, Signer of the Declaration of Independence," accessed September 24, 2011; www.barefootsworld.net/johnhart.html.

Beal, Scott C. "Anderson Family History," (2004), accessed September 25, 2011; http://familytreemaker.genealogy.com/users/b/e/a/Scott-C-Beal/PDFGENE5.pdf.

Bear's Mill online, "History of the Mill," accessed January 12, 2012; www.bearsmill.com/history.html.

The Broad Axe Tavern online, accessed September 24, 2011; http://www.broadaxetavern.com/.

Brownsville, Pennsylvania online, "Pittsburgh might amount to something if it weren't so close to Brownsville," accessed September 26, 2011; http://web.me.com/rpday/background/brownsville.html.

Byers, Michele S., Executive Director, New Jersey Conservation Foundation. New Jersey Today online, "Saving Colonial History at Petty's Run," accessed September 26, 2011; http://njtoday.net/2011/09/23/saving-colonial-history-at-petty%E2%80%99s-run/.

Champaign Convention and Visitors Bureau online, "Cedar Bog Nature Preserve," accessed September 26, 2011; http://champaignoh.com/stay-and-play/recreation/49.html.

Chiltern Open Air Museum online, "The Victorian Blacksmith," excerpted from *The Countryman Cottage Life Book*, Fred Archer, ed. (David & Charles, Publishers, 1974), accessed December 17, 2011; http://www.coam.org.uk/images/workshop%20pdf/KS1workshops/Blacksmith.pdf.

City of Lancaster, Pennsylvania online, accessed September 26, 2011; www.cityoflancasterpa.com.

City of York, Pennsylvania online, "City of York — The First Capital of the United States," accessed September 25, 2011; http://yorkcity.org/history.

Colonial Williamsburg online, "The Fences of Williamsburg," accessed September 26, 2011; www.history.org/history/teaching/cwfences.cfm.

Conner Prairie Interactive History Park online, "Clothing of the 1830s," accessed January 12, 2012; http://www.connerprairie.org/Learn-And-Do/Indiana-History/America-1800-1860/Clothing-of-the-1830s.aspx.

Conservatree online, "A Brief History of Paper," accessed January 12, 2012; http://conservatree.org/learn/Essential%20Issues/EIPaperContent.shtml.

Cumberland Road Project online, "Scenes from the Old National Road, Allegany County, Maryland," accessed September 26, 2011; http://www.cumberlandroadproject.com/maryland/allegany/photo-pages/the-narrows-photos1.php.

Dictionary.com.

East Vincent Township, Pennsylvania online, "East Vincent Churches," accessed September 24, 2011; www.eastvincent.org.

The Free Dictionary online, accessed September 26, 2011; http://www.thefreedictionary.com/Indeterminateness.

Google Maps.

Google Translate.

Historical Marker Data Base online, "Wilson's Store: Store of Three Wonders," accessed September 26, 2011; http://www.hmdb.org/marker.asp?marker=4932.

Historic Ships in Baltimore online, "USS *Constellation*," accessed January 12, 2012; http://www.historicships.org/constellation.html.

Kramer, Sandy. Texian Legacy Association online, "TLA Lady's Page: Starting Out: Women's Clothing — 1830s Style," accessed January 12, 2012; www.texianlegacy.com/ladys.html.

Lancaster County, Pennsylvania Government online, "A Self-Guided Walking Tour Along Historic King Street from Penn Square to Broad Street" accessed September 26, 2011; http://www.co.lancaster.pa.us/lancastercity/lib/lancastercity/east_king_walking_tour.pdf.

Library of Congress online, "Chronicling America," accessed September 25, 2011; http://chroniclingamerica.loc.gov./lccn/sn85026350.

Maryland Geological Survey online, "Maryland's Highest Waterfalls and Mountains," accessed September 26, 2011; http://www.mgs.md.gov/esic/fs/fs9.html.

Maryland State Highway Administration online, "Wilson Bridge 1817–19," accessed September 26, 2011; http://www.sha.state.md.us/Index.aspx?PageId=272.

Moore, Robin. "The USS *Preble*, Sloop of War 1838–1863," accessed January 12, 2012; www.tfoenander.com/preble.htm.

Mountain Zone, Maryland mountain peak information online, "Fairview Mountain Summit," accessed September 26, 2011; http://www.mountainzone.com/mountains/detail.asp?fid=6587456.

Northampton Historical Society online, "Endangered White Bear: A History of the Spread Eagle Inn," accessed September 24, 2011; http://www.northamptontownshiphistoricalsociety.org/SpreadEagle/SpreadEagle_history.pdf.

Bibliography

Ohio Department of Geological Survey online, "Glacial Map of Ohio: Ohio Department of Natural Resources, Division of Geological Survey," 2005, accessed September 26, 2011; http://www.dnr.state.oh.us/portals/10/pdf/glacial.pdf.

Ohio Department of National Resources online, "History of Ohio Canals," accessed January 17, 2012; http://ohiodnr.com/water/canals/canlhist/tabid/3285/Default.aspx.

Ohio Hiking Trails: Miami and Erie Canal online, "Miami and Erie Canal History," accessed January 12, 2012; http://www.hiking.ohiotrail.com/trails/canal-history.htm.

Penn State College of Agricultural Sciences, Penn State Extension online, "The Soils of Pennsylvania Part 1, Section 1: Soil Management," accessed September 26, 2011; http://extension.psu.edu/agronomy-guide/cm/sec1/sec11a.

Reading Railroad online, "RDG Co.–A Breif (sic) History," accessed September 26, 2011; www.readingrailroad.org.

Rootsweb's World Connect Project online, "Hunterdon Co, NJ, inhabitants 1700–1800," accessed September 25, 2011; http://wc.rootsweb.ancestry.com/cgi-bin/igm.cgi?op=GET&db=fredericlathrop&id=125879.

Rutgers School of Arts and Sciences, Department of Earth and Planetary Sciences online,"Geology of the Newark Rift Basin," accessed September 26, 2011; http://geology.rutgers.edu/103web/Newarkbasin/NB_text.html.

Science Encyclopedia, accessed September 26, 2011; http://science.jrank.org/pages/3035/Germ~Theory.html.

The Seven Stars Inn online, "History of the Seven Stars Inn," accessed September 23, 2011; www.sevenstarsinn.com/history.htm.

Snyder, Dr. Cliff, Southeast Director of the Potash and Phosphate Institute. Back to Basics: The Premiere Soil Fertility Information online, "Efficient Fertilizer Use Manual," (February 2006), website accessed September 26, 2011; http://back-to-basics.net/efu/pdfs/pH.pdf.

Taylor, Archer. *Western Folklore*, 22 "Number Six" (1963) pp. 193–94, accessed January 12, 2012; www.folkmed.ucla.edu.

Tobacco News and Information online, "Economic Aspects of Tobacco during the Colonial Period 1612–1776" accessed September 26, 2011; http://www.tobacco.org/History/colonialtobacco.html.

Trenton City Directory for 1859 online, accessed September 25, 2011; http://trentonhistory.org/Directories/1859dir.html.

Trenton City Directory for 1844 online, accessed September 26, 2011; http://www.trentonhistory.org/Directories/1844DIR.html.

Trenton Historical Society. *A History of Trenton 1679–1929: Two Hundred and Fifty Years of a Notable Town with Links in Four Centuries.* (Princeton, NJ: Princeton University Press, 1929), accessed September 24, 2011; http://www.trentonhistory.org/1929history.html.

UCLA Folklore Archives, "Indigo," accessed January 12, 2012; www.folkmed.ucla.edu.

United States Department of Agriculture, Agriculture in the Classroom online, "A Look at West Virginia Agriculture," accessed September 26, 2011; www.agclassroom.org/kids/stats/westvirginia.pdf.

Fips, Bots, Doggeries, and More

United States Department of the Interior, National Register of Historic Places Registration Form, Leitersburg Historic District, WA-I-174, November 5, 2003, accessed October 5, 2011; *http://www.msa.md.gov/megafile/msa/stagsere/se1/se5/020000/020900/020917/pdf/msa_se5_20917.pdf.*

United States Department of the Navy — Naval Historical Center Online Library of U. S. Navy Ships, accessed January 12, 2012; *http://www.history.navy.mil/photos/sh-usn/usnsh-p/penna.htm.*

Wikipedia.org.

Index

Ackerman, Amelia Smith 80
Acuff, Ann 4, 48, 96
Addison (Petersburgh), Pennsylvania 3, 36, 93, 111, 112
Auburn Prison System 80

Bank of Urbana 15
Bexley, Ohio 106, 116, 117
Biddle, Nicholas 72
Blacksmith 16, 20, 41, 57, 89, 90, 126, 130, 141
Bots 31, 83
Bridge(s) 1, 8, 18, 25, 26, 29, 32, 33, 38, 39, 42, 43, 45, 46, 47, 48, 51, 55, 56, 59, 68, 77, 91, 92, 93, 94, 95, 96, 105, 107, 109, 110, 114, 129, 130, 140, 142
Broad Axe Tavern 4, 48, 49, 51, 96, 123, 130, 141

Canal(s) 1, 2, 21, 25, 27, 41, 42, 45, 46, 49, 56, 68, 69, 74, 76, 77–78, 95, 101, 107, 126, 138, 140, 143
Capsicum 82
Church 2, 21, 50, 53, 64, 67, 83, 84, 96, 99, 100, 106, 138, 142

Clay, Henry 32, 72, 74
Columbus, Ohio 3, 15, 18–19, 21–22, 24, 77, 79, 91, 100, 101, 106, 117, 124, 126, 129, 137, 138, 139, 140
Corn 13, 14, 15, 17, 25, 28, 29, 31, 32, 35, 40, 45, 47, 56, 57, 92, 97, 114
Crop(s) 1, 2, 32, 69

Democratic political party 53, 74, 75

Evans, Oliver 69, 70–71

Fairfield Inn 118
Fip (phip) 27, 92
Folk remedies 2, 5, 31, 82–83, 129
Frankford Arsenal 63, 99

Gallatin, Albert 76
Geological formations 29, 34, 35, 39, 44, 54
Groff, C. C. 8–9

Hagerstown, Maryland 43, 44, 94, 112, 130, 139
Hamilton County, Ohio 7, 9, 91, 126, 138
Harrow 51, 60
Hartman, Charles 8

Hebron, Ohio 24, 25, 92, 107
Hill, Jediah 7, 14, 19, 21, 31, 45, 51, 52, 53, 54, 55, 56, 57, 59, 60, 62, 64, 65, 66, 67, 78, 96, 98, 131, 133, 134
Hill, Eliza Hendrickson 7, 14, 15, 17, 19, 21, 50, 52, 53, 54, 56, 57, 59, 60, 62, 63, 64, 65, 66, 68, 89, 96, 97, 99, 131, 132, 133, 134
Hog scalder 64
Horse(s) 1, 2, 14, 15, 21, 24, 28, 30, 31, 32, 35, 37, 39, 41, 44, 45, 46, 48, 51, 54, 55, 56, 59, 60, 61, 63, 66, 67, 81, 83, 91, 94, 95, 98, 111, 114, 116, 129, 130, 140
Hotel(s) 1, 3, 8, 15, 21, 25, 29, 44, 46, 48, 50, 59, 92, 94, 95, 98, 108, 109, 112, 115, 117, 120, 121, 124, 129

Illness 1, 14, 15, 28, 29, 30, 32, 34, 36, 52, 65, 88
Indigo 31, 83, 143

Jackson, Andrew 72, 74, 77, 92
Jacksonian 25, 46, 48, 75, 92, 101, 138
Jefferson, Thomas 76

Land speculation 72

Lehman's Mill, Hagerstown, Maryland 113–114

McClure, Dr. Robert 32
McIlroy, Carl 84, 120
Mill(s) 1, 2, 5, 7, 8, 9, 13, 15, 16, 24, 26, 27, 28, 34, 40, 43, 47, 52, 54, 55, 57, 65, 66, 69–71, 90, 91, 94, 97, 98, 100, 105, 109, 113, 114, 121, 124, 126, 139, 140, 141
Monroe, James 77, 93
Mount Healthy, Ohio 3, 7, 8, 9, 89, 96, 112, 140
Mount Pleasant, Ohio 1, 3, 7, 89, 105, 124
Mountain(s) 34, 35, 37, 39, 40, 41, 44, 45, 46, 51, 54, 93, 94, 110, 111, 142
Myrrh 31, 82–83

National Road 2, 3, 16, 18, 23, 24, 25, 30, 31, 32, 38, 39, 40, 42, 69, 74, 76, 77, 78, 91, 92, 93, 94, 100, 101, 106, 107, 109, 110, 111, 114, 116, 117, 121, 125, 126, 129, 137, 138, 139, 140, 141, 142
Number 6 31, 32, 82, 129

Ohio Bicentennial Wagon Train 109, 116
Ohio Historical Society 90, 91, 106
Ohio Lunatic Asylum 21, 23

Panic of 1837 73, 99
Petersburgh (Addison), Pennsylvania 35, 36
Philadelphia Navy Yard 2, 61, 63, 87, 112, 139
Philadelphia, Pennsylvania 4, 45, 46, 47, 48, 51, 52, 55, 58, 59, 60, 61, 62, 63, 79, 87, 93, 96, 97, 98, 99, 100, 117, 120, 121, 130, 137, 138, 139, 140
Pinney, Levi 18, 91, 126, 132

Pinney, Mrs. Levi (Maria) 21, 91, 126, 132

Ohio Penitentiary 19–21, 129

Railroad train 45, 46, 48, 56, 68, 78, 95, 96, 110, 112, 130, 143
Revolutionary Soldiers Cemetery 2, 49, 83–84, 101, 119, 120
River(s) 4, 15, 21, 24, 25, 26, 27, 30, 32, 35, 41, 45, 46, 48, 51, 52, 54, 60, 62, 68, 77, 78, 81, 82, 92, 95, 97, 109, 111, 124
Rogers, Henry, Jr. 1, 7, 78, 91, 96, 125, 131, 132
Rogers, Henry, Sr. 7, 126
Rogers, Phoebe Burnett 7
Rogers, Rachel Maria Hill 7, 14, 15, 17, 19, 21, 28, 34, 36, 53, 55, 56, 57, 59, 60, 62, 64, 65, 66, 68, 131
Rogers, Wilson T. 8

S Bridge 107, 109, 110
Saint Clairsville, Ohio 25, 77
Searight, Thomas B. 33, 92, 93, 94, 120, 121, 140
Second Bank of the United States 72–74, 101
Seven Stars Inn 96, 119, 120, 130, 143
Shinplaster(s) 15, 90
Sickness (horse) 30, 32, 39, 40
Smith House Antiques 25, 80–82, 108, 109
Specie Circular Act 15, 62, 73
Stanton's Mill, Garrettsville, Maryland 114

Tavern(s) 4, 19, 25, 28, 29, 33, 34, 36, 39, 40, 41, 44, 45, 46, 48, 49, 50, 51, 60, 61, 62, 63, 68, 75, 80, 81, 82, 90, 91, 92, 93, 94, 95, 96, 105, 106, 108, 109, 110, 111, 112, 113, 114, 116, 118, 120, 121, 123, 125, 126, 129, 137, 138, 139, 140, 141
Threshing machine 66, 99
Toll gate(s) 24, 28, 41, 107
Trenton, New Jersey 4, 48, 52, 53, 54, 55, 56, 58, 59, 62, 64, 65, 96, 97, 98, 99, 100, 117, 121, 122, 129, 137, 138, 140, 143

US Mint 62, 99
US Route 40 25, 93, 106, 107, 110, 111, 112, 114, 115, 121
USS *Constellation* 112, 113, 142
USS *Dale* 61, 87–88, 112
USS *Pennsylvania* 87

Van Buren, Martin 74, 75

Washington, George 76
Wheat 17, 28, 29, 31, 35, 78, 92
Whig political party 18, 74–75, 101
Widow Bevins' tavern 41, 130

Y Bridge 26, 91, 92, 109, 140
Young Millwright and Miller's Guide (1795) 69

Zane's Trace 110
Zanesville, Ohio 25, 26, 27, 77, 81, 91, 92, 107, 109, 110, 129, 140